THE NONFICTIONIST'S GUIDE

THE NONFICTIONIST'S GUIDE

ON READING AND WRITING CREATIVE NONFICTION

Robert Root

ROWMAN & LITTLEFIELD PUBLISHERS, INC.
Lanham • Boulder • New York • Toronto • Plymouth, UK

ROWMAN & LITTLEFIELD PUBLISHERS, INC.

Published in the United States of America
by Rowman & Littlefield Publishers, Inc.
A wholly owned subsidary of The Rowman & Littlefield Publishing
Group, Inc.
4501 Forbes Boulevard, Suite 200, Lanham, Maryland 20706
www.rowmanlittlefield.com

Estover Road, Plymouth PL6 7PY, United Kingdom

British Library Cataloguing in Publication Information Available

Library of Congress Cataloging-in-Publication Data

Root, Robert, 1942-
   The nonfictionist's guide : on reading and writing creative nonfiction/
Robert Root.
      p. cm.
   Includes bibliographical references and index.
   ISBN-13: 978-0-7425-5617-1 (cloth : alk. paper)
   ISBN-10: 0-7425-5617-4 (cloth : alk. paper)
   1. Reportage literature—Authorship. 2. Prose literature—Authorship.
3. Creative writing. I. Title.
PN3377.5.R45R66 2008
808'.042—dc22

                                                      2007027303

Printed in the United States of America

⊚™ The paper used in this publication meets the minimum requirements
of American National Standard for Information Sciences—Permanence of
Paper for Printed Library Materials, ANSI/NISO Z39.48-1992.

For Tim and Paul,
husbands, fathers, and friends,
with love and admiration

"I write entirely to find out what I'm thinking, what I'm looking at, what I see and what it means. What I want and what I fear."

—Joan Didion

"The discipline of a writer is to learn to be still and listen to what his subject has to tell him."

—Rachel Carson

CONTENTS

PREFACE

This is a book about reading and writing nonfiction of a particularly literary kind. "Nonfiction" is a vague term. In its widest interpretation it encompasses all uses of language that are not the traditional three literary genres of fiction, poetry, and drama. Such an interpretation includes instruction manuals, research reports, lab notes, hospital records, term papers, journalism, grocery lists, road signs, and card catalogues, to name but a few. This book will not use the word in that sense. "Nonfiction" is a word of limited value to writers or readers unless they have some shared specific definition in mind. I'll elaborate on my definition in the chapter on the nature of nonfiction, but for now I'll simply point out that, when I say "nonfiction" in this book, I mean what we usually refer to as "creative nonfiction" or "literary nonfiction." Those terms are slippery enough in their own rights that I'll mostly avoid them hereafter.

Here, nonfiction, the fourth genre, refers to such forms of writing as the personal or familiar or reflective essay, the memoir in short or long forms, personal narrative reportage of travel and place and exploration and investigation, the kind of individual-anchored cultural criticism that may also be identified as expressive critical writing or personal academic discourse. It refers to nonfiction that may be narrative, lyrical, dramatic, meditative, expository; that may be expressive, poetic, referential, persuasive; that may be intimate, confessional, reportorial, critical, analytical, argumentative; that may be any combination of these. It is nonfiction that Mike Steinberg and I, in the introduction to our anthology, *The Fourth Genre: Contemporary Writers of/on Creative Nonfiction*, claim can be identified by these common elements: personal presence (the author's self as spectator or participant, whether on the page or behind the scenes), self-discovery and self-motivation, flexibility of form (the tendency for the form to arise from the content rather than the content to be contorted to fit an inverted pyramid or five-paragraph or similarly prescriptive model), veracity (to paraphrase Annie Dillard, rendering the real world coherent and meaningful either analytically or artistically), and literary approaches (drawing on narrative techniques also used in fiction or lyrical language also used in poetry or dramatic rendering of scenes or cinematic uses of pacing and focus).

A reader may feel—justifiably—that my definition of nonfiction is not as narrowly delineated as it might be, but one of my concerns has been to help writers avoid being hemmed in by boundaries imposed by critics, scholars, textbook authors, and other writers—the willingness to construct walls around a subject and patrol it against trespassers is a human weakness too eagerly accepted by academics, educators, and, yes, creative writers. I want to define the form by the evidence of what's created in the genre; I also want to stand aside and watch imaginative nonfictionists contribute to its expansion and mutation.

The book is composed of two braided strands. Each main chapter may be considered as notes toward what might be called a "Poetics of Nonfiction," focused on looking at elements of nonfiction in ways that help readers appreciate the aesthetic elements of the genre; a section following each chapter, labeled "Notes for Nonfictionists," extends the discussion in that chapter by offering suggestions and recommendations about composing strategies and approaches and craft issues more specifically directed toward writers. This division, however, is not meant to suggest that one section is exclusively for readers and the other exclusively for writers—writers need to be informed, observant readers, and readers can gain from reading as writers do.

I see this book as part of a continuing conversation about nonfiction that I've been having for a while now with other writers as well as other teachers and other scholars of the form. Most of the chapters originated as essays on the genre. The essay, as proposed and practiced by Michel de Montaigne, is a literary form governed not by rules and restraints but by impulses and intentions. *Essai* in French means "attempt" or "test"; to *essayer* is to try. I think that the most fundamental basis from which to write the fourth genre is the instinct of the essayist, the desire to answer Montaigne's questioning motto: "What do I know?" This book, then, is an invitation to "essay" nonfiction by considering both how some writers have already done it and also how other writers might attempt it.

For those who wish to know more about the way we write nonfiction now I hope that these reflections will be informative and provocative. For those who aspire to or already do generate work in the fourth genre, I hope these chapters will prove to be practical and productive. For both readers and writers I hope to offer a reliable nonfictionist's guide.

ACKNOWLEDGMENTS

The Nonfictionist's Guide is the result of years of conversations and conferences with students, teachers, and colleagues around the country, as well as a host of convention papers, public addresses, workshops, and articles. The many people I am indebted to for deliberate guidance and inadvertent insights are literally too many to name. Nonetheless I must single out a few. Michael Steinberg and I have been involved in a number of stimulating and fruitful projects over the years, particularly the Traverse Bay Teaching Workshops, which culminated in our book *Those Who Do Can: Teachers Writing, Writers Teaching*, a great many panel discussions and even more panel proposals, and the multiple editions of our anthology, *The Fourth Genre: Contemporary Writers of/on Creative Nonfiction*, which grew out of simultaneous development of nonfiction courses at different universities. I'm grateful for our long partnership. I've also benefited from being the interview/roundtable editor for *Fourth Genre: Explorations in Nonfiction*, which Mike founded and continues to co-edit with David Cooper. My unique role is to talk to writers in interviews and roundtables or to edit interviews and roundtables moderated by others. This experience has enriched my understanding of our common field, and I'm grateful to Mike, David, interviewees Kim Barnes, Scott Russell Sanders, and Marjane Satrapi, and roundtable panelists Lisa Knopp, Simone Poirier-Bures, Natalia Rachel Singer, Michele Morano, Marilyn Abildskov, Judy Copeland, Carole de St. Victor, John Calderazzo, Kristen Iversen, and Michael Gorra. At Central Michigan University I had the good fortune to share an office with John Dinan for nearly three decades, to briefly co-edit the *Language Arts Journal of Michigan* with him, and to continually gain from his conversation and classroom example. In addition I talked about teaching writing with Susan Schiller, Linda Peterson, Matt Echelberger, and Carol Sanford and worked in courses and on theses with such fine writers as Sarah Dickerson, Mary Beth Pope, Emily Chase, Sheryl Grant, Amy Nolan, Angie Fenton, Sandra Smith, Jim Conway, Lisa Hadden, Amy Solinski, and Bill Milligan. As a writer at writers' workshops I gained a great deal from Gretel Ehrlich, Garrett Hongo, Don Stap, and William de Buys. I am most appreciative of time spent with Elizabeth Dodd, Reg Saner, Shari Caudron, and Steve Wingate.

I should also acknowledge that this book was aided by earlier opportunities to present ideas and materials on teaching and writing at conferences of the Associated Writing Programs, the Conference on College Composition and Communication, the Conference on the Literature of Region and Nation, the University of New Hampshire Conference on "Breaking the Mold: Experimenting with Nonfiction," the University of Warwick conference on Teaching Writing in Higher Education: An International Symposium, the Michigan Council of Teachers of English, and the AEPL Annual Conference in Estes Park, Colorado, on "Mapping Nonfiction: Inspiring a New Sense of the Terrain." Some of this material was the subject of addresses to the Writer's Studio at the Box Factory for the Arts in St. Joseph, Michigan, the MFA in Creative Nonfiction Program at Goucher College, and the Muskegon (Michigan) Area Teachers of English. Portions of chapters in this book that started out as convention papers, talks, or addresses also appeared in considerably different form in literary and professional journals and textbooks. Those earlier versions and trial runs include:

"Beyond Linearity: Writing the Segmented Essay." *Writing on the Edge*, 9:2 (Spring/Summer 1998): 27-34.

"Captioning and Capturing the Past." *Statement* 42:1 (Summer 2005): 9-15.

"Collage, Montage, Mosaic, Vignette, Episode, Segment." In *The Fourth Genre: Contemporary Writers of/on Creative Nonfiction,* ed. Robert L. Root Jr. and Michael Steinberg. New York: Allyn & Bacon, 1999: 258-68.

"The Experimental Art." *JAEPL: Journal of the Assembly for Expanded Perspectives on Learning,* 9 (Winter 2003-2004): 12-19.

"Locating a Nonfiction of Place." In *Landscapes with Figures: The Nonfiction of Place,* ed. Robert Root. Lincoln: University of Nebraska Press, 2007: 1-12.

"The Memoirist as Essayist." *Fourth Genre: Explorations in Nonfiction,* 6:2 (Fall 2004): 127-29.

"Naming Nonfiction (a polyptych)." *College English,* 65:3 (January 2003): 242-56.

"Of Nonfiction and Time." *Language Arts Journal of Michigan,* 16:1 (Spring 2000): 51-57.

"Scenes, Stanzas, Segments and the Essayist's Art." *Fourth Genre: Explorations in Nonfiction,* 3:2 (Fall 2001): 216-22.

"This Is What the Spaces Say." In *Conversations About Writing: Eavesdropping, Inkshedding, and Joining In,* ed. M. Elizabeth Sargent and Cornelia Paraskevas. Toronto: Nelson, 2005: 309-11.

"Variations on a Theme of Putting Nonfiction in Its Place." *Pedagogy* 4:2 (2004): 289-95.

"Why Don't You Collage That?" *Writing on the Edge* 12:1 (Fall/Winter 2001): 21-26.

I am grateful to those editors for providing a space for me to carry on this conversation about nonfiction.

The part of my life that is not centered on writing and teaching has been blessed by the presence in it of Sue, Tom, Becky and Paul, Caroline and Tim, and Zola, Ezra, and Louie. I have a lot to be grateful for.

1

THE NATURE OF NONFICTION

One of the things I've learned over years of teaching and writing is that all discussions are determined by underlying assumptions. No matter what we're talking about, no matter what we actually know about whatever we're talking about, we operate out of some set of underlying assumptions, hopefully researched and reasoned but often—perhaps usually—instinctive or intuitive or impulsive. Our opinions on whatever may be the topics of the day tend to emerge out of predispositions, prejudices, and unexamined attitudes. When I talk to other writers or editors about creative nonfiction, as I have often in recent years, I find the conversation depends on deep-seated reactions to the word "creative" or to the word "nonfiction"; I also find reactions largely predictable, depending on which tradition—of the three major "disciplines" that can lay some claim to the "field" of creative nonfiction—the person I'm talking to identifies with: journalism, creative writing, or composition/rhetoric. I have enough experience writing books to know that readers—including publishers, editors, and reviewers—haven't always read the book an author thinks he wrote; it's discouraging, for example, to be criticized about how successful your book is as a biography when, in fact, you never had any intention of writing a biography.

So if I'm to write a book about writing nonfiction, the prudent thing to do at the outset is explain the assumptions that underlie what *I'm* talking about. In regard to nonfiction that will involve answering three fundamental questions: What is it? Why do writers do it? What kind of writing comes out of it? These are the questions I hope to answer under the headings of meaning, motive, and margins.

MEANING

I'm a nonfictionist. It's symptomatic of the field in which I work that dictionaries don't acknowledge such an occupation. If you type "poet" or "dramatist" or "novelist" into your computer, your automatic spellchecker ignores them, but if you write "nonfictionist," a squiggly red line appears under the word. I could say I'm an essayist or a memoirist, respectable enough titles, but either of those terms excludes all the non-essayistic/non-memoiristic nonfiction I write. That strikes me as nonsense.

Part of the problem is using old words for new things. Take a term like "creative nonfiction," for instance, an unexceptional term for those of us familiar with it but not necessarily acceptable to all its practitioners, let alone its critics. Both of the words are problematic to begin with; together they can sometimes evoke outrage. "Nonfiction," to some people, is written and spoken only with a hyphen ("NON-fiction") and includes everything that is not fiction—not only essays and memoirs and journalism and reports but, to be strictly literal, this page, my shirt, my granddaughter's toys, the tree outside my window, all poetry and all plays. "Creative" always gets someone's dander up, not so much when applied to "creative writing" but often when *not* applied (by inference) to other forms of nonfiction—say, this page, someone's research report, someone else's memo. Many people assume that "creative" and "nonfiction" are incompatible terms and that nonfiction is a strictly non-creative form of writing—

just the facts, ma'am. (Unfortunately, among the most vocal of those striving to keep creativity out of nonfiction are English teachers who rail against the first person singular and the personal voice and the use of narrative in composition papers at the same time that they assign readings in Annie Dillard, E. B. White, Henry David Thoreau, Alice Walker, George Orwell, and Virginia Woolf, creative nonfictionists all.)

Most dictionaries offer little help getting a handle on nonfiction. The word itself is neither evocative nor self-defining. Imagine having labeled television as "non-radio" or cinema as "non-publication" or a saint as "non-prophet." Efforts to coin a catchy alternative in jargon-laden academic disciplines leave us nonplussed, produce only nonce words. The term "literary journalism" is too limited, excluding so much nonfiction that is also literary but not journalistic; the term "creative nonfiction" is too oppositional, implying a need to distinguish it from "non-creative nonfiction." That's the problem with this "non" business—it reduces everything to dichotomies: fiction opposed to nonfiction, creative opposed to non-creative, and so on. In this *post*-age, where literary theorists distinguish contemporary work from that of earlier ages chiefly by being *beyond* them—*post*-modern, *post*-structuralist, *post*-process—perhaps we should simply declare ourselves to be now *post*-nonfiction. We're so beyond dictionary definitions of nonfiction that to say "Nonfiction is not just 'not fiction' anymore" is to state the obvious. It may even be *post*-obvious. Taking our cue from critical theory, let's simply *revision* the definition completely, make it non-derivative and pro-descriptive. Abandon etymology—forget the "non"; forget the "fic"; keep the "tion" only if it doesn't get in the way. Let's use the word we already have as if it has always meant what we now use it to mean.

In that spirit, as an attempt to clarify the way we write nonfiction now, I offer the following alternative definitions:

Nonfiction n.

1. the written expression of, reflection upon, and/or interpretation of observed, perceived, or recollected experience;

2. a genre of literature made up of such writing, which includes such subgenres as the personal essay, the memoir, narrative reportage, and expressive critical writing and whose borders with other reality-based genres and forms (such as journalism, criticism, history, etc.) are fluid and malleable;
3. the expressive, transactional, and poetic prose texts generated by students in college composition courses;
4. (obsolete) not fiction.

I often give the first two definitions to my students when they ask, "So, like, what *is* nonfiction?" The definitions give us a way of narrowing the field.

The first definition has two advantages: First—and most important—it tries to define nonfiction in terms of what it *is* rather than in terms of what it *isn't*. Second, it potentially sets the norm from which definitions of other genres divaricate. In order to use it for their genres, fictionists and poets and dramatists will need to add some qualifiers. Those other genres usually deal with imaginary, invented, or fabricated events presented in a way to make them *seem* observed, perceived, or recollected, or, conversely, they present observed, perceived, or recollected experience *by the means of* imaginary, invented, or fabricated scenes and characters. Perhaps nonfiction is the first or primary genre from which the other genres branch off according to their modes of representation. I suspect that language was developed to serve the needs of observed, perceived, or recollected experience—the nonfiction motive. For example, "There are wooly, mammoth creatures at the waterhole." Or: "Let me explain how your mate was gored by a wooly mammoth." Or: "This is what we know about wooly mammoths that will help us find them." Fiction, poetry, and drama are patinas slathered on reality and need reality as their foundation; for nonfiction, reality is its essence, its outward show as well as its inner core.

The second definition links to the first but tries not only to be suggestive about the varieties of literary nonfiction but also to be inclusive rather than exclusive. I think definitions ought to arise from what already exists—be drawn from the characteristics and qualities of things that are—rather than to describe an abstract ideal and impose unnecessary and unrealistic limitations on concrete possibilities. It's the difference between letting an essay be whatever it wants or needs to be and forcing it to be a five-paragraph theme.

In the third definition I'm simply picking a fight. English departments tend to divide discourse into "personal" and "academic," and privilege the latter over the former ("creative" discourse they ignore or isolate altogether). For me, terms like "personal" and "academic" aren't very useful descriptors. Isn't the opposite of personal "impersonal"? Shouldn't the opposite of academic be "non-academic"? But then we're back to defining things by what they're not. Moreover, such terms generate a false dichotomy. The personal and the academic are not in opposition to begin with. My students only get in trouble with "academic" writing—or "non-academic" writing, for that matter—when they leave the "personal"—their commitment, their engagement—out of their works-in-progress. I prefer the terms I've taken from the functions of discourse identified by James Britton and the London Schools Project. Expressive, transactional, poetic—these terms cover very nicely the range of writing not only students but also working writers do.

In the fourth definition I'm merely stating the post-obvious.

I don't believe for a moment that these definitions are, well, definitive, and I'd be interested in knowing how others would change them or add to them or substitute something else for them. But for my students, in composition classes as well as in creative nonfiction classes, and for me, as a practicing nonfictionist, the first definition works particularly well. It doesn't leave out the writing we're already composing and reading; it doesn't make us worry about what we aren't but lets us focus on what we are; it defines what we do.

MOTIVE

For some time now, as I've been exploring and examining and generating nonfiction, I've been surprised but pleased to find myself circling back around toward ideas that, many years ago, triggered my conversion from Restoration comedy specialist to specialist in composition theory and practice. These ideas were articulated by such varied figures as Ken Macrorie, Peter Elbow, James Moffett, Janet Emig, Donald Murray, and James Britton. Increasingly I find myself arguing for nonfiction as a form that satisfies expressive, transactional, and literary aims in writing equally well; it is not simply a literary kind of journalism or a reportorial kind of creative writing or a creative extension of composition. Such perspectives make nonfiction simply an option for writers in other forms or genres rather than a motive for writing in the first place. Nonfiction is not simply an option of style or format or attitude; it's a perspective on the world, and its texts are composed by writers animated by the nonfiction motive.

The writer chooses nonfiction as a medium because of a desire or a need or a drive to understand a portion of the world and to record and respond to that understanding. Those portions of the world the writer hopes to understand may include, perhaps, such topics and ideas as these: the way a method for determining longitude was first discovered; the way a birch bark canoe is constructed and how its construction relates to its use; what the circumstances were behind the famous photo of the flag raising on Iwo Jima and what became of the flag raisers; what forces were at work in her parents' marriage and why she had the childhood she did; what led to his addiction to alcohol or gambling or sex or baseball or Japanese anime; why he or she was able to lead a happy, productive, and largely uneventful life (this last is a memoir sorely in need of being written). The challenge in subjects like these is not knowing where you'll end up and having to make sense of the information you uncover, whatever it is, rather than imagining the information and inventing the outcomes.

The nonfiction motive is the individual writer's need to know or to understand a specific, limited topic. Any time we separate the writer from that motive, we swing the text away from nonfiction and allow it to veer in two problematic directions: into the realm of indifference, where we don't care what we really know as long as we have something to hand in—this leads not only to too many unsuccessful composition assignments but also to too many academic articles—or into the realm of fantasy, where we concentrate less on what we know or understand and more on what we wish or what we fear or what we can imagine without regard to evidence—this leads not only to fiction and, alas, more academic articles but also to outfits like Fox News (the people who put the contempt in contemporary journalism). In nonfiction the writer has to deal with the real world, has to make an effort to come to terms with reality, with truth. The nonfictionist thinks, "Here's a situation: What does it mean? What significance does it have? How can I make sense of it? How can I most accurately convey its meaning when I learn it?" The nonfictionist doesn't intend to take the information and shape it into whatever she feels like shaping it into or contriving a way to contort it to fit an agenda; instead, the nonfictionist's motive is always, at bottom, a desire to understand the information with which she's confronted, to uncover its shape, to follow where it leads her.

Without the nonfiction motive, writers get no internal checks and balances on their own honesty, no incentive to investigate, explore, observe, compare witnesses, and analyze all the evidence, no commitment to comprehend or to extend that comprehension to readers. Before you can write nonfiction that truly matters to readers, it has to matter to you. You have to have the nonfiction motive.

All of this is meant to indicate that the motive behind writing nonfiction is real and significant; if missing or falsified, the work becomes, at the least, counterproductive and, at the worst, annihilating. More important, if we don't examine our own motives in writing, we can't be certain we are writing for any real or substantial reason.

How we approach what we write makes a great difference in what results. That's often a problem with writing assignments not only in writing classes but also in subject matter courses—a student's motive in writing is to clear a hurdle or fulfill a requirement or complete an assignment or master a skill rather than to acquire and express knowledge or to share insight and information. The results are often detached, disengaged, insincere. If, among working writers, writing really matters, is written for real motives within the writer, why wouldn't "motive" be essential to apprentice writing or novice writing?—that is, why wouldn't those writers also need the motive to really comprehend and to really communicate?

MARGINS

A few years ago, for a convention panel on nonfiction where I was severely constrained by the time allotted for my presentation, I read a brief, energetic prose polyptych about the meaning of white spaces between segments in "disjunctive" essays (the basis for the section of this book titled "This Is What the Spaces Say"). Afterward, a friend came up to me and said that he was a little perplexed by it; it seemed to him that the piece was very lyrical and yet it was also highly academic. "What," he wanted to know, "do you call that kind of essay?" I hadn't thought up a term for what I had done, but, using the hints he'd provided, I invented a label on the spot. "It's a lyrical academic essay," I said. Laughing, he objected, "But there is no such thing." Laughing, I replied, "Of course there is. You just heard one."

It was one of those unexpected interchanges that startled me by making me suddenly aware of something I didn't know I knew. It helped me realize that nonfiction is not simply a conforming art—it's also an experimental art. It heightened my awareness of how often it's necessary to ignore the impulse to force the essay to fit a pre-arranged structure and, instead, to let the structure arise from the essay—to, in effect, let the essay (or memoir or cultural criticism or what have you) become whatever it needs to become. It may have to follow a familiar, conventional structure, but alternatively it may have to become a completely unique literary form, alone in its own subgenre—sui generis. Creative nonfiction, in particular, abounds in experimental forms. I've also come to believe that our definitions need to be determined by our practices rather than insisting on the reverse—that our definitions determine our practices.

How then can you locate the margins, the limits, the boundaries, of nonfiction? Like so many topics, we need to identify things by their centers, their cores, because the more we move toward the margins the more distinctions blur and territories overlap. When, in Colorado, I drive up to Estes Park from Boulder, I can see the mountains on one side and the plains on the other, but it's difficult to pinpoint a decisive dividing line between them. Terrain doesn't shift instantaneously from one biome to another, nor do literary forms. The center of nonfiction, I believe, is located at the point where the nonfiction motive emerges, where the expressive urge to identify, record, or respond to experience arises. That urge, to borrow from James Britton, is the matrix out of which personal and interior writing, informative and expository writing, aesthetic and literary writing all emerge and pursue their own paths. From that center nonfiction stretches and spreads in many directions and, over varying distances, transmutes itself into subtly different terrains, some more expressive, some more transactional, some more literary. We may not know we've left the rolling plains of the nonfiction heartland until we're deep into some other landscape—the craggy mountains of poetry, the misty marshland of fiction, the arid deserts of journalism, the labyrinthine forests of scholarship. All discourse begins where we are, in the landscape we really inhabit, and expresses itself first in nonfiction, the effort to express, reflect upon, or interpret observed, perceived, or recollected experience. The variations in genres and subgenres of discourse, from the most flagrant to the most subtle, are extensions from that center, varying from the slightest shifts in climate or elevation or habitat to starkly different terrains, even semi-detached peninsulas or possibly, because of rising literary water levels, distant islands set off from the mainland. Some forms of nonfiction—the "non-creative" or "non-literary" (even "anti-creative" and "anti-literary")—may be distinguished by their tendency to submerge, camouflage, or minimize overt authorial presence and to foreground, highlight, or maximize aspects of subject matter, as journalism, history, biography, and more academic or "transactional" forms of science and nature writing do. While extremes may exist at either end of these extensions, the distinctions among forms can be measured on a sliding scale of engagement, authorial presence, rhetorical accessibility, and distance from the core of the nonfiction definition.

Let me anchor these ideas more concretely with examples. Since I mentioned the mountain west earlier, I'll draw on several works ostensibly written about the same general region. I'll begin with Isabella Bird's *A Lady's Life in the Rocky Mountains*, partly written in 1873, when Bird was temporarily living in Estes Park. Bird, later identified as Isabella Bird Bishop, wrote a number of travel narratives over a long and peripatetic life, but her Rocky Mountain book came early. She had been encouraged to travel for her health, went off to Australia, the Hawaiian (or Sandwich) Islands, and the United States, and wrote long, detailed letters to her sister Henrietta in England narrating and reflecting upon her experiences. She initiated the letters without the intention of book publication; edited versions of those letters later appeared serially in *The Leisure Hour*, a British popular magazine, and then became the text for *A Lady's Life in the Rocky Mountains*, published in 1879. While a letter-writer may or may not have the intention of publishing more widely than her specific correspondence, the intention of communicating to another person no doubt influences the nature of the letters—expands the narrative, heightens the description, reveals motivation and attitude and response. Isabella Bird came to Estes Park, climbed Long's Peak, and toured a good portion of the Front Range. Her letters to her sister were a way of recording that experience, responding to it, and, eventually, rehearsing the book she would write about it. This is a part of the nonfiction motive—this desire to preserve the memory of one's experiences. While any piece of writing is an interpretation of events and thoughts, nonfiction is the genre in which one strives for the most direct and most accurate preservation of experience. In Isabella Bird's letters she was simultaneously expressive, recording her own experiences, and transactional, informing her sister about them. This intimacy between writer and reader carries over into the published book. *A Lady's Life in the Rocky Mountains* is valuable for its record of a particular place in the western landscape at the dawn of its European-American occupancy and development as well as for its insight into a particular individual intelligence inhabiting the experience. As a locus for nonfiction, it's a very good place to start.

Isabella Bird's writing is a good example of the expressive matrix transforming itself into transactional writing, and the book is a charming and evocative portrait of the Colorado frontier in the period the author was riding through it. In a sense it's nonfiction at its most stripped down, though even more basic is journalkeeping. The impulse to journalize—to record the day's events, respond to experiences, puzzle through one's own reactions and spontaneous thoughts—is certainly the most expressive of literary forms, and most frequently produces writing only ever read as it is being written, by the author alone. But often it leads to more developed, more publishable writing. For example, *The Solace of Open Spaces* by Gretel Ehrlich began as journal entries composed in Wyoming and then sent in letters to a friend in Hawaii. Ehrlich, a poet and documentary filmmaker, had originally come to Wyoming to do a short film on sheepherding and returned, grieving, to work as a sheepherder. The journal entries were simply her way of investigating her emotional and physical life, the necessary means of immersion into her new circumstances. Eventually, between 1979 and 1984, the journals-cum-letters evolved into essays and the essays evolved into the book, published in 1985.

Like Bird's book Ehrlich's too is an expressive work, richly revealing of her inner life, but it is also highly literary, drawing on her propensity toward lyrical expression. Bird and Ehrlich share an inclination to write about their experiences in various terrains—each wrote other books about other locations—and to draw upon the approaches of their early work—Bird uses the "letters from a traveler" narrative often in her writing and Ehrlich frequently incorporates journal entries or journal-like passages in her essays and books. Bird became a dedicated travel writer, someone setting out in the world—she also wrote books about Hawaii, Japan, Persia and Kurdistan, China, Tibet, Korea, and the Malay Peninsula—to report back on what she discovers wherever she wanders; Ehrlich became more of an essayist or a memoirist, and her investigations are more inward even in the most remote terrains—she has written on Japan, China, Greenland, and the Arctic, as well as on the American West. Bird evolved from a primarily expressive writer into a deliberately transactional writer—eventually she was setting forth on her journeys in order to write about the places she went, rather than writing about the places she went as a way of expressing her observations about them—and Ehrlich evolved into a literary writer, a self-conscious essayist, from her expressive journalkeeping, which has been a regular part of her literary strategy all along.

With these two examples I seem to be claiming for nonfiction the motives of self-expression and literary expression exclusively, but I think the range is broader than that. A nonfiction writer may want to make sense of something that he may not have experienced directly, as personal event, but may have experienced intellectually, as impersonal reflection. The connections between these kinds of circumstances are not always transparent, but often the writer makes the connection for us. When Terry Tempest Williams, a writer from Utah, saw Hieronymus Bosch's triptych "The Garden of Earthly Delights" at the Prado in Madrid, she recognized the end panels of Paradise and Hell as pictures that hung over her bed when, as a child, she visited her Mormon grandparents. The connection was the trigger for her desire to fully comprehend the painting. She set about to thoroughly examine the triptych and also to explore the forces behind her reactions to the painting, not only in its artistry but also in her personal and family history. The result was *Leap*, a book that tumbles together expressive, transactional, and literary aims. It is an imaginative inhabiting of Bosch's painting, an investigation of Mormon theology, and a reminiscence of her own upbringing and current spirituality.

Even without that overt personal connection, a writer's determination to follow through on curiosity or interest may grow out of circumstances or impulses other writers don't have about the subject. John McPhee is always my example of how a writer can turn his interest in any subject into a fascinating piece of writing for a reader who may not be initially interested in it. For example, *Oranges*, his exploration of the way fresh oranges become orange juice concentrate, a topic that grew out of curiosity prompted at his breakfast table, was so engrossing that a reviewer wrote of it, "You may come to the end of it and say to yourself, 'But I *can't* have read a whole book about oranges!'" Similarly, people with no interest in geology may have read his entire series of four books on the geology of North America as they were published individually over a period of years, and then have read, as I did, the entire series a second time when they were combined with a fifth section into his magnum opus, *Annals of the Former World*. One volume of that series is *Rising from the*

Plains, a book principally about the geology of Wyoming and the formation of the Rocky Mountains but also a profile of the geologist David Love and a history of his family.

The personal shows up in McPhee's writing—he very often travels with an expert in the field he's studying (a geologist, a park ranger, a farmer, an art dealer) and the narrative of those travels and conversations and the trajectory of the author's learning from experts are very much a part of the structure—but it is almost never central and in some cases hardly makes an impression on the reader. Yet even in works where the author has no overt presence on the page, as a character, interlocutor, or observer, the author's motive is individual, distinctive, determined largely by McPhee's interests or experiences.

Even nonfiction that seems at first blush more academic doesn't occur in a vacuum (as much as many academic writers try to make it appear). One writer who has been particularly open about centering her academic writing in expressive contexts is Jane Tompkins. Her classic essay "At the Buffalo Bill Museum, June 1988," published in her thematic collection *West of Everything: The Inner Life of Westerns*, recounts her visit to an interlinked complex of museums at the Buffalo Bill Historical Center in Cody, Wyoming. The trigger for her speculations and analyses is her need to understand her own reactions to what she's seeing. The result is a work of cultural criticism that also works as a personal essay. Similarly, Rebecca Solnit, in *River of Shadows: Eadweard Muybridge and the Technological Wild West*, often uses her own experiences as jumping off places for wide-ranging investigations of highly theoretical, often technical subject matter, such as the blend of research into art, photography, landscape, and history that fills the book.

With Tompkins and Solnit we are starting to push the boundaries of creative nonfiction over the border into academic scholarship; with McPhee we are highlighting creative nonfiction that doubles as literary journalism and that may be claimed by journalistic writers as much as, or even more than, literary writers. As I suggested, I don't know where the cut-off points in these subdivisions of nonfiction are and, as may by now be obvious, I'm not interested in resolving such issues.

Simply perusing the work on the mountain West by Isabella Bird, Gretel Ehrlich, Terry Tempest Williams, John McPhee, Jane Tompkins, and Rebecca Solnit, any reader can develop a vague sense of the kind of terrain nonfiction takes in and appreciate the breadth of space between its boundaries. We can also recognize the difficulty we face when we try to locate its outer margins.

———∞∞∞———

In a sense these issues of meaning, motive, and margins are an effort to start to imagine a poetics of nonfiction. More specifically, they are all heads of an answer to the question, What do I mean when I talk about nonfiction in this book? These are the assumptions that underlie the following chapters. I expect that those chapters will build on, expand from, sometimes clarify, probably complicate, and possibly contradict these assumptions. I'm suspicious of prescriptive approaches to writing, though I believe a great deal is knowable about it, and I don't claim to have answered all issues that might emerge. My knowledge of nonfiction, of the art and craft and act and labor of writing, is a work in progress and my assumptions are open to revision if they hinder writing in any way. But I expect that what follows will make it easier for writers with a nonfiction motive to become more committed to, and more capable of, expressing, reflecting upon, and/or interpreting observed, perceived, or recollected experience. That, simply put, is the intention of the book and my assumption about what it has to offer the reader.

NOTES FOR NONFICTIONISTS: LAST WORDS FIRST

Both as a writer and as a teacher I've noticed that sometimes aspects of writing need to be spelled out and sometimes aspects of writing can simply be intuited. From project to project, from writer to writer, it isn't predictable which approach will work. For that reason, I try, as much as possible, to draw on both strategies, to count on both systematic and spontaneous approaches. The intuitive or spontaneous part of writing occurs when in the course of our reading or observing or doing, ideas and memories and reactions come to us unbidden because whatever is happening at the moment triggers responses we didn't foresee. The systematic part of writing occurs when we deliberately provoke or at least invite a response by putting ourselves in the path of likely reactions.

In terms of this opening chapter, this means that reading about meaning, motive, and margins may have prompted an unexpected response or a connection in the reader. That's the intuitive, impromptu aspect. If it did provoke a response or a connection for you, I recommend that you put the book down right now, grab a pen and paper (or grab a keyboard and open a file), and start jotting down what you're thinking about and why you guess you're thinking about it. Don't stop to formulate anything—just let the words flow and follow where they lead you for the next ten to twenty-five minutes.

If you don't feel that impulse, it doesn't mean you haven't been responding to what you're reading—the systematic approach is a good way to explore what you might be connecting to in the further recesses of your mind. (The systematic approach is also a helpful expansion upon and exploration of whatever the intuitive approach surfaces.) Reacting informally to what you've read is a deliberate act if you set out simply to examine what you've noticed and to question yourself about how it applies to you.

Two key elements of this chapter invite a systematic consideration: the definition of nonfiction and the explanation of motive. Consider the definition first. If "observed experience" refers to what you've done or witnessed or what you would like to observe or witness, make a list of ten observed or observable experiences of interest to you. Then put a star in front of three items on the list that most capture your attention and briefly write for three to five minutes apiece about what each item involved or might involve. Observed experience is the stuff of personal essays and immersion articles, and by this little exercise you can identify potential projects in those kinds of writing. "Perceived experience" refers to what you've read or been a spectator for; it's the stuff of cultural criticism and expressive academic discourse and investigative reportage. Put yourself through the same listmaking and focusing exercises here. "Recollected experience" is the stuff of memoir and personal narratives and cultural reportage. Once again, put yourself through the same activities.

Then consider the nonfiction motive: "the need to know or understand a specific, limited topic." It might be personal, intimate, subjective; it might public, social, objective; it might involve a specific discipline or event or artifact or experience. What topics come to mind for you? What would you be motivated to pursue, given your inclinations and interest? Write for ten minutes about what you uncover.

All of this is exploratory, merely informal probing of your own mind, but perhaps something will emerge here that will lead you to an eventual writing project. Even if it doesn't, you've begun to investigate how your reading connects to your interests and to figure out what might be the focus of the nonfiction you could write. You'll also begin to recognize what happens when nonfictionists launch themselves into writing projects.

That's a good place to start.

Throughout this book I'll try to avoid giving blanket advice suitable for all occasions, but it might be appropriate here to say something more about the writing life that might give nascent nonfictionists the courage to persevere. These are also the things I would like to say at the end of this book, so I'd encourage nonfictionists to reread this section after they read the last page of the final chapter.

Writing is hard enough to begin with, publishing is generally discouraging even when successful, and marketing is a special skill completely unrelated to writing. We all need some sort of nudge to keep moving from time to time. So here are the most universal practical recommendations I can come up with.

- If you're going to write, you have to read. Reading other writers connects you to a community of similarly motivated people; reading the kinds of nonfiction you're interested in writing makes you aware of possibilities and options and variations—it fosters a sense of how writers use language and structure and strategies of pacing and rhythm and balance.

- If you're going to write, you have to write regularly. If you keep a journal, a diary, a daybook, fieldnotes, or a weblog (blog), or if you simply rely on multiple drafts, regular writing develops a kind of momentum—a writer in motion stays in motion, a writer at rest often has a hell of time getting back into motion. Writing in small increments daily is more productive than writing in infrequent marathon sessions once in a blue moon.

- If you're going to write, expect the writing to uncover—discover— things you didn't know you knew and things you need to know before you can complete the writing. Expect to do some sort of on-site or source research with every project. Expect to make connections with things you didn't know were related to your subject.

- If you're going to publish, know what's being published, where it's being published, and who publishes it. As much as possible be familiar with the magazines, literary journals, and publishing houses where you send proposals or manuscripts. Investigate the protocols of publishing in guides like *The Writer's Market* and Jeff Herman's *Guide to Book Publishers, Editors, and Literary Agents*. Keep alert to calls for submissions in *The Writer's Chronicle* and *Poets and Writers* and online at www.webdelsol.com. Expect to have your work rejected and to have to hunt for editors who are on the same wavelength as you are.

- If you're going to publish, connect with a circle of first readers, more than one individual who can respond and react to what you're writing—sometimes certain people are simply the wrong readers for a certain work and other times certain people know exactly what you're trying to do and can suggest ways for you to do it more successfully. Take more than one writing class, or attend a writer's workshop or a writer's conference, or form a writer's group locally or online.

- If you're going to write, pay attention to what writers in the field you're working in say about their writing processes, their approaches to their genre, their ways of wrestling with words and texts. Find advice to copy down, and consult what you've copied from time to time, because every writer has to be reminded of things he or she already knows or should know about writing, and admonitions from other writers are good ways to get back on track.

Lastly—and this is something you'll hear often when you ask advice from writers—write first for the sake of the writing, for what the writing does for you and for the rewards inherent in writing well. "The whole duty of a writer," E. B. White wrote, "is to please and satisfy himself, and the true writer always plays to an audience of one." To put it another way, the writing always has to serve the writer's needs first, and the writer has above all to serve the writing as best she can.

2

NOT THE DESIGN
OF THE AUTHOR

Simon Winchester writes narrative nonfiction about historical intellectual achievements. Halfway through *The Map That Changed
the World,* an account of William Smith's nineteenth-century efforts
to depict the geology of Great Britain, Winchester re-creates a scene
when he himself was six years old, playing on a beach with other
children from his boarding school, and found a fossil ammonite. Just
such fossils imbedded in sedimentary layers of rock helped William
Smith to recognize the relative ages of geological strata. At the close
of that chapter, Winchester revisits the site of his childhood discovery and walks the coastline with a new awareness, generated by his
study of Smith's discoveries, of the rock formations that make up the
bluffs along the shoreline. Failing to find another ammonite but now
understanding better where the one he found in childhood came
from, he writes,

> As I walked back up the cliff to the parked car it occurred to me that
> my hero and I were now subtly connected by this single small lozenge
> of limestone and calcite, by the smooth and silkily beautiful physical
> object that he had once held in his hands, much as I had done all
> those years later.

Winchester refers to the fossil ammonite as not simply "a four-ounce reminder" of vanished tropical oceans in England but also "a cozy link between the past and the present, between the extremes of the ultramodern and the ultra-ancient."

In such a scene the author reveals the transforming possibilities of creative nonfiction. Despite its scientific and historical subject matter and its dependence upon thorough analysis and synthesis of research materials, this particular book was written because of an object its author discovered on a beach in childhood and his willingness to transform curiosity into knowledge. The individual writer is always implicated in what she or he writes. Creative nonfiction allows—even encourages—the writer to follow the thread of connection back to that first implicating impulse; it also authorizes disclosure of such implications, invites accounts of just such epiphanies as Winchester has had on that beach.

That moment records the transformation of the author's understanding of his subject. The historical nonfiction Winchester writes belongs to a class of books about the impact on the modern world of individuals and discoveries that we take for granted—think of works on longitude, the Oxford English Dictionary, the Northern Lights, the compass, cod, daylight savings time. Researching and writing changes the way the author sees the world; it leads the writer, and subsequently the reader, to a new understanding of the way the world once was and transforms our comprehension of the way the world is now. The best of these kinds of books are involving and intimate and immerse us in the periods they record. In this regard, despite their "academic" subjects, they are unlike most academic writing, which endeavors to keep the reader and the writer at a detached distance. The further back you stand from the subject—as writer or reader—the slighter the transforming possibilities of the encounter, but in creative nonfiction those possibilities are heightened.

Like Winchester, I too have written a book about a person who lived in the middle of the nineteenth century, the author of a journal that had virtually no effect on the world. The journal of Mrs. C. C. Douglass for the year 1848 begins with this New Year's Day entry:

Mr. Douglass brought in this Book to day and presented it to me, saying, as we should probably be moving about some the coming year it would be well to keep a journal of our migrations. I very willingly acceded to this wish, but shall not attempt to carry out the design of the Author by keeping a regular daily journal but will endeavor to record incidents as they may occur.

When I first read that passage, in 1989, I was struck by Mrs. Douglass's use of the phrase "the design of the author" and its implication of intentionality, self-consciousness, aesthetic ambition. Though she is willing to be a journalkeeper, Mrs. Douglass insists that she will not be an author. Certainly a daily journal, particularly one like hers that she didn't write in daily, depends less on deliberate craft and more on happenstance and coincidence for its "design."

In August 1848 Mrs. Douglass and her husband traveled to Isle Royale, a remote island in Lake Superior, where he was to supervise a mining company and they were to spend the winter cut off from the mainland. In spite of Mrs. Douglass's intentions her journal grows somewhat livelier and more concrete, more thoughtful and revealing, in its final months. On Christmas day she writes:

The contrast in the manner of our spending the day is quite different from last Christmas Day, then among our friends in Ann Arbor, now, on a remote and lonely island, but I forbear to repine, we are happy here, even in this solitude, but should be happier if we could communicate with our friends. We have as many of the comforts of life here, as we should enjoy in almost any place, many more than one would suppose that had had no experience in this new country. We have as yet a plenty of fresh meats, such as, Beef, Fish, Fowls, Rabbits, &c. &c, together with as good vegetables as one would wish to find in any place, also a sufficiency of nick-nacks. In short everything for our health and comfort.

The experience of living on Isle Royale has transformed Mrs. Douglass from someone daunted and unnerved by the prospect of her "migrations" to someone confident and intrepid in the face of experience. Though her journal opens with a poem of "serious reflections" about "the departure of the old year and the commencement of the new" and closes with a similar poem about "the fleetness of time" and the way "time by moments steals away," the year of journalkeeping and travel has brought her to a more knowledgable place about these matters—her philosophizing is grounded in experience. In that regard her journal of their migrations is also a journal of her transformations. She has achieved a design whether she intended one or not.

Shortly after I read Mrs. Douglass's journal the first time, I proposed to edit, annotate, and introduce the journal for publication. An easy and enjoyable job, I thought—the journal was, after all, short, partly set on a place I loved, and offered me experience for an editing course I wanted to teach. I had an easy design as an author—look up information to provide endnotes on the places and persons and events she mentions, transcribe, copyedit, and proofread the manuscript, and write an introduction providing historical-biographical background. The Clarke Historical Library card catalogue identified the author as "Douglass, Lydia Reed Smith" and noted that the journal was written in her first year of marriage, when she was sixteen. Her husband, Columbus C. Douglass, who was twenty years older, had been a prominent Michigan citizen. I found considerable information about him and about mining on Isle Royale and about his life on the mainland in the 1850s but no references to Lydia earlier than the late 1850s to early 1860s, when their children were born. I wondered why they hadn't had children for over ten years, especially in that era, but in time I found his grave, her grave, the graves of three of their children. I'd thought about Lydia and written about Lydia off and on for years when I finally decided to look in official records for the date of their wedding.

I'll condense my shock and confusion here, though in life it was extended and prolonged. I learned that Columbus married Lydia in 1856 and that previously, in 1847, he had married a woman named Ruth Edgerton. The 1848 journal was not Lydia's but Ruth's. It had been read in manuscript by various mining scholars and attributed to Lydia Douglass for years, but, other than a solitary gravestone in Detroit, it was the only artifact remaining of Ruth Douglass's life and

I was the only one who knew it. Somehow I had acquired responsibility for this woman's identity; I was the only person who could restore it to her. My relationship to this material, to this author, was transformed, from that of academic editor to that of a conservator or caretaker, the ad hoc executor of her estate.

But the transforming possibilities don't end there. Richard Holmes, the biographer of Coleridge and Shelley, has observed that, in addition to "the gathering of factual materials," part of "the essential process of biography" is "the creation of a fictional or imaginary relationship between the biographer and his subject . . . a continuous living dialogue between the two as they move over the same historical ground, the same trail of events." He describes this dialogue as "a steady if subliminal exchange of attitudes, judgments and conclusions," and insists that, though "the subject cannot really, literally, talk back" to the biographer, "the biographer must come to act and think of his subject as if he can." Holmes believes that "a degree of more or less conscious identification with the subject . . . a type of hero- or heroine-worship, which easily develops into a kind of love affair . . . is an essential motive for following in the footsteps . . . of someone else's life through the physical past." He insists, "If you are not in love with them you will not follow them—not very far, anyway," and refers to this relationship as a "naïve form of love and identification."

Part of the difficulty I had accepting the change from one journal keeper to another was the bond of attachment I had already formed with Lydia. I felt a little like Roxane in *Cyrano de Bergerac*, discovering that Cyrano and not Christian had written the letters she treasured. I felt like Christopher Reeve's character in *Somewhere in Time* or Dana Andrews's character in *Laura*, haunted by an image in a portrait of someone I'd never met. One day, after finally visiting Ruth Douglass's grave in Detroit, I returned to my apartment in Mt. Pleasant with a rental video of *Somewhere in Time* and watched it again, intending to allude to it in my writing about Ruth Douglass. Unexpectedly, it transported me back in time, to my first viewing of the film, in a period when I had been intensely involved with someone physically distant and romantically unattainable. The film had devastated me then, surfacing my own loneliness, longing, and loss, and it stunned me on this second viewing, reviving all those feelings and linking them inexplicably to my relationship to this nineteenth-century journalkeeper who had died in 1850. The moment transformed my sense of my role in this project—confounded and complicated it. It made me realize the degree to which the projects we choose, seemingly of our own free will, are grounded, often imperceptibly, in our own values, experiences, past lives. It was not my design as an author to become so enmeshed in this project, but on reflection it seems to me that I have been similarly involved and implicated in all the other projects that have mattered to me, even if they have not been projects of such emotional intensity.

When Ruth Douglass talks of "the design of the author" she means the intention to craft a text; she does not intend to *compose* a journal but rather expects to function as a conduit through which events will dictate content. She will not be an author but a scribe, a transcriber of experience. But writing, as exercises in freewriting and journaling and similar extemporaneous forms of composing teach us, doesn't let us keep our distance, especially when we write often and at length. It transforms us by giving us access to places we never were or by changing us back into someone we once were. It also transforms our intentions and designs by bringing us to a better perspective on what we understand, what we have created.

The Map That Changed the World, Simon Winchester's book, is a narrative nonfiction blending scientific history and biography; *Recovering Ruth,* my book, is an intellectual memoir braiding my travels with historical and biographical backgrounds of Ruth Douglass's life. Winchester is seldom on-stage in his book, except for the chapter I cited, and I am either on-stage or just off-stage throughout mine. Both of our books are grounded in research but Winchester's, despite its basis in personal experience, is almost entirely about the fruits of his research while mine, despite its frequent focus on background information, is more about the process of my research—it is the most personal book I've yet written. That these two works of creative nonfiction, one a history, one a memoir, have so much in common suggests, to me at least, some things that seem essential about the nature of writing.

Nonfiction is grounded in the writer's personal experience—the more writers resist getting in touch with that groundedness, the less useful the writing is to those writers. The disengaged, disinterested writer relies too readily on a detached or dishonest design. Nonfiction is also dependent upon research, on an understanding of background, whether the subject is intimately connected with or remote from the writer's experience—the more nonfiction writers avoid anchoring their writing in actuality, the less useful it is to the reader. Without feeling obliged for its accuracy the writer either intentionally or inadvertently evades honesty. Whether memoir or history, the more we close off the possibility of transformation in the writer, the more we negate the possibility of transformation in the reader.

This isn't a new idea—teachers of composition used to know that writing is as much *for* learning as *about* learning, that writing is a means of discovery as well as a means of communication; they also used to try to get their students to realize that—but it seems to be an idea that writers need to be reminded of every so often, that writers have to rediscover for themselves from time to time. You can't write about what you've learned until you've learned something, you can't communicate until you discover something you need to communicate. No matter how remote the subject is from the writer's personal life, the writer has to connect with it somehow before a reader can connect with it.

One of my students, Sheryl Grant, once told me, "I think creative nonfiction is as much about the craft of living as about the craft of writing. It seems that good writing is just as much about being honest with ourselves as it is about writing well—technically and emotionally." She was then writing memoir and nature narrative, and learning that, as a nonfiction writer, she had to be willing to be taken somewhere she didn't intend to go in order to arrive somewhere she needed to be. She was discovering that, whether she began with the design of the author—the intention to craft a text—or not, once she let herself be open to the transforming possibilities of writing, the design would emerge from the evolving text.

Sheryl's discoveries about her writing echo my own. She wrote, "I prefer to write creative nonfiction because it helps my life make sense, not just my writing."

I say, "Me too."

NOTES FOR NONFICTIONISTS:
THE DESIGN OF THE AUTHOR

Writing begins with engagement and exploration. To be an effective writer of nonfiction you have to accept these twin elements. A writer needs to have a commitment to the subject matter, a sense of involvement that is not simply a desire to communicate something but is instead—or in addition—a willingness to discover and accommodate whatever emerges from the writing. If you don't want to discover anything, if you aren't committed to the writing or the subject, you won't get far. In John Jerome's classic phrase from *The Writing Trade*, writers need subjects that give them "gear teeth for their interests," some purchase that propels them forward through the process. I've seen writers elect a topic that seemed to them safe or easy or certain and then watched the writing fall apart on them. It's what Sue Lorch discovered writing a boring paper about a painting that she thought was boring before she started writing about it; it's what Vivian Gornick is saying, in *The Situation and the Story*, when she points out that describing a situation isn't enough—doesn't get either writer or reader anywhere—and that the writer has to find the story, the significance, the reason the subject needs to be written about; it's what Gail Sher is driving at in *One Continuous Mistake: Four Noble Truths for Writers* when she observes, after pointing out that writing is a process, that the writer may not know what the writing is about until she reaches the end of the process. "I write to find out what I didn't know I knew," Robert Frost said, and many other writers have echoed him. If you don't want to know what you didn't know you knew, don't write— writing is a means of discovery as well as a means of communication. Engagement and exploration go hand in hand.

Writers are often urged to keep a writing log or a project journal as a safe place to muse about the process and progress of their writing projects. It's a safe place because you aren't writing for others there or composing a work to go public with but merely having an impromptu conversation with yourself about the writing you're doing or hope to do. There you spontaneously write to yourself about what you're planning, how the writing's going, what stumbling blocks have appeared, how the work completed so far might be altered in the future. The writing journal is a good place to think through what you're doing, check in with yourself about its progress, dodge your editorial self, and do an end run around the author self having difficulty with more deliberate composing.

It's also a good place to examine intentions and designs as you go along. You might ask yourself early on: What about this project interests or excites me? What do I hope to learn? What do I hope to accomplish? How does this connect to what I need to know about myself? How does it connect to what I need to know about this subject? Why do I want to know this? What will I need to learn, to know, before I can complete this project? These are questions you hope to answer as concretely and as honestly as possible—it's a journal; you're the only one you're fooling if you don't—but they're also questions where the answers are likely to be tentative at the outset. You may wrap up the journal entry thinking, "This is as much as I know so far and it's good enough for now."

If you commit to the project and launch yourself into it, you can continue to check into those issues, try out new answers to earlier questions, answer new questions as they arise, and, as you progress, adjust your understanding of what you're doing and why. When the project's completed to your satisfaction, at least to the point where you feel you've done all you need to do, it wouldn't hurt to review where you wound up and notice the way you got there. Such an overview will likely reinforce your confidence in your ability to improve upon what you've written over a period of time. It will certainly argue against committing to a particular design—a rigid set of intentions for a project—so fully that it controls the content of what you compose and, instead, confirm the idea that the design you expected to follow is likely to have been suggestive rather than defining. A sense of engagement and a spirit of exploration complement one another effectively. As the writer and teacher Donald Murray used to urge writers, it's important to "expect the unexpected" and "invite surprise" as you write.

3

THE
EXPERIMENTAL ART

Sometimes it's tempting to imagine that nonfiction is a predictable art, that perfect nonfiction could be produced by some infallible method—a formula, a pattern, some sort of mold. A mold is ideal if you want to reproduce something that is identical to something else that's been produced before. My grandfather had a mold in the basement into which he poured molten lead to manufacture six identical fish-shaped sinkers, all equal in size, shape, and weight. That's why we have molds, that assurance of uniformity. That's why we have formulas, so we can identically reproduce medicines, prescriptions, motor oils, detergents, and other chemical concoctions. That's why we have recipes, so we can re-create the taste and texture of meals someone else has tested in the past. If the goal of working from a mold is uniform manufacture—the exact replication of an idealized model—then molds and recipes and formulas and dress patterns and house floor plans are very good things to have. They make us able to predict the outcome.

Sometimes writers ask for molds, something they can use to achieve predictable end products. Sometimes they want to know the page length or word length requirements and the acceptable number of references in order to make a paper fit the academic mold; sometimes they want to fall back on the cosmetics of a lead and the insertion of a specific number of quotes from sources in order to make an article fit the journalistic mold. The measure of success in working from a mold is the degree to which one can predict that the thing manufactured will look like everything else out of that same mold.

I once was given a cookbook with recipes submitted by average people in which there were at least a hundred recipes for tuna noodle casserole. They were all essentially the same recipe except for minute variations in measurements and ingredients—the canned tuna might be flaked or chunk, the packaged egg noodles thin, medium, or wide, the condensed soup cream of celery or cream of mushroom, the peas canned or frozen. With these slight differences identical recipes were reproduced on page after page, like a massive photo album of lead fishing sinkers from the same mold. Sometimes writing workshops and courses and guide books approach writing as if its goal were to compose the equivalent of a tuna noodle casserole cookbook, to produce a catalog of identical lead sinkers. But that isn't the goal. Writers can't predict the sense and shape of their writing; instead, they need to experiment with meaning and experiment with design. Nonfiction is an experimental art.

Rather than selecting a mold and making the molten material conform to it, the nonfictionist needs to determine the design demanded by the material. We're dealing with reality here; unlike fiction or drama or poetry, the material of nonfiction is always what's already out there to begin with; it's not something we manufacture out of whole cloth—it's something we have to make sense of *by means of* an essay or a memoir or an article. We experiment when we explore the material, when we gather and research information, when we try to make connections and determine relationships and see what fits and what doesn't. The shape of a work of nonfiction arises from its subject; its design emerges as the *result* of composing rather than from *rules* for manufacturing it. It's rather like Michelangelo's approach to sculpture, starting with a block of marble, then "liberating the slave in the stone"—that is, discovering what the marble tells him ought to emerge from the sculpting. In a similar way, nonfiction discovers its form in the subject. Sometimes the form that emerges is a strict chronology or a step-by-step process. Sometimes it's a movement from particular to general or from general to specific. These are traditional patterns, to be sure, but no writer first decides to write in such a pattern and then locates material that will fill it; instead, the writer works with the material and tries to discern an appropriate shape as understanding unfolds. Sometimes experimentation will lead the writer to traditionally linear or conjunctive forms; I think a Montaigne essay, in its meandering stream of consciousness, is following the course of its own experiments with meaning. But sometimes experimentation will lead the writer to a design so untraditional that it seems to have never been used before. Nonfiction is an experimental art because it experiments with meaning as part of the discovery process and it experiments with form as part of the presentation process.

REFLECTION RAG

Let me offer up a specific essay to serve as illustration. Consider Christine White's "Reflection Rag: Uncle Joe, Roberto Clemente, and I," published in the Spring 2002 issue of *Fourth Genre*, a journal of nonfiction. White begins "Reflection Rag" with this short paragraph:

> So much happened so quickly after Uncle Joe died. The tempo changed. This new rhythm blew aside the curtain and there it was, this other order of things that lies beneath or beyond; a hidden stage where we play out our lives and strange bedfellows mingle and the orchestra plays ragtime and spirits stand in the wings, feeding us lines, leading us home.

The essay is rich, complex, intricate, multi-faceted, and the paragraph is a prelude, an introduction, an overture, to the movements which follow. It is a segmented essay, and each segment has a separate title—"Exit Uncle Joe," "Enter Roberto Clemente," "Arriba! Arriba!," "What the Music Means," "Grace Notes," "Hypertime," and so on. The essay begins with a segment on the death of her uncle Joe, raised in Pittsburgh but dead in Colorado, and the succeeding segments follow an unpredictable thread of connections. While waiting for Uncle Joe's funeral, the narrator attends a ragtime music festival and hears a rag titled "Roberto Clemente." It is named for the Puerto Rican right fielder for the Pittsburgh Pirates who played for the baseball team when the author was growing up in Pittsburgh.

"Reflection Rag," her essay, goes on to explore the unexpected connections between the author, her uncle Joe, Roberto Clemente, Scott Joplin, and ragtime music. It also serves as meta-nonfiction, because it is also about the author's discovery of the synchronicity in these connections as she researches and writes the essay. White explains that, though she doesn't entirely understand why, she feels a bond to Clemente and a bond with the rag named for him. She tells us,

> I believe the universe works this way. Uncle Joe and Roberto Clemente and I, we were destined to interact with one another. It doesn't matter that Joe died last week and Clemente died over twenty-five years ago and I'm still around. That's how time works sometimes.
>
> And, I am to find out, that's how writing is sometimes. I start out chasing one story and then another story starts to chase me. I want to write about Uncle Joe but Roberto Clemente jumps in. And then other forces become involved. You see how it is. Sometimes a writer has no choice.

At the end of this segment she writes, "I tell you, it's the best part of writing sometimes, to play hide and seek this way with the past, to live things again, and to write about ragtime."

As the essay progresses we learn more about Roberto Clemente, including the bias he faced as a baseball player and the circumstances surrounding his death in an airplane crash as he was returning to Puerto Rico; as it happened, Clemente died on Christine White's birthday. We learn more, as well, about Uncle Joe, including his difficult personality, his prickly relations with his wife and son, his finally coming to accept the granddaughter whose Latina mother his son was afraid to commit to because of his father's bias against Hispanics. We learn too about Scott Joplin and ragtime music, how the "left hand on the piano plays the stride bass or *basso continuo*, keeping the pulse with the characteristic *oom pah* beat" and the "right hand plays the melodies and rhythmically works against the left hand." We learn how Joplin's wife refused to have "Maple Leaf Rag" played at his funeral, how his final composition was titled "Reflection Rag."

In a segment titled "No Simple Stories" White writes: "I think it would be nice to write a simple story for once but there are no simple stories. Just simple ideas and little insights that take a long time in telling. All of this back and forth, the meshing of the pieces of this ragtime puzzle, is how I sort through the ideas that fill my head when I write." Later she reminds us, "I told you before. We really don't choose our stories. When we're hot, our stories chase us until we catch them." The essay illustrates this, as if it is being written while we are reading it.

As I've suggested, the theme of "Reflection Rag" is synchronicity, the obscure but suddenly obvious connections between people and objects and events that we do not realize are there, have been there all along. How can one make sense of synchronous connections? How can one work through them? David Roberts wrote the rag "Roberto Clemente" after seeing a film about him and wanting to commemorate him somehow. Christine White explains, "As a musical composition, 'Roberto Clemente' has four musical themes or melodies. These themes vary and repeat, vary and repeat, returning with nuances and interpretations determined by the composer and the performer." Then she adds, "To me this sounds a lot like life." To that response I can only add that, to me, this sounds a lot like her essay. She herself has written what may be the only nonfiction rag; she has made "Reflection Rag" not only the title of both a Joplin tune and her essay but also a new form for nonfiction.

Moreover, Christine White was right about the way that writing works. Think of her statement, "All this back and forth, meshing the pieces of this ragtime puzzle, is how I sort through the ideas that fill my head when I write." For a moment see that image of someone moving around pieces of a puzzle, experimenting with the placement of one piece in juxtaposition to several others, looking for a place where its shape locks against another shape or at least suggests the shape of a missing piece that might link the two pieces that she has. In nonfiction we continually work with pieces of puzzles and the rules say we can only play with what we're given—we can't manufacture linking pieces to complete the design, like a novelist can; instead, we have to make sense of only the pieces we've turned face up. The puzzles you purchase in a store are easier to complete—the pieces were cut deliberately from an original whole, made to go back together, constructed so that they fit back into their original mold.

But nonfiction puzzles never show you an original image that can be eventually reconstructed from the pieces you have before you; some pieces will always be missing, most pieces will never fit tightly with another piece, and the pieces you're trying to arrange into a whole may not have come from the same original—perhaps they came from several or perhaps from no entire original whole at all. You not only have to experiment with where the pieces go in order to imagine how they fit together, you may also have to experiment with their arrangement in order to get anyone else to see what you see in the pieces before you. In order to help the reader understand what the writer feels about synchronicity and ragtime, it may be necessary to write a nonfiction rag.

THE MALLEABILITY OF CONTEMPORARY NONFICTION

One of the elements of contemporary creative nonfiction that makes it an experimental art is its malleability in the face of an author's need to invent a completely new design to accommodate the subject she's writing about; it demands as well that the author find a way to guide readers through a form they can't have had any experience with. A ragtime essay may reveal to another writer or to any reader the possibilities inherent in an experimental art—the way a structure may be created or invented to meet a need—but, unlike such formulaic models as the "five-paragraph theme" and the "inverted pyramid," it doesn't provide a template, a boilerplate, a ready-made mold to be filled.

Contemporary creative nonfiction abounds in examples of idio-syncratic experimental forms. Some, like Nancy Willard's "The Friendship Tarot" or John McPhee's "The Search for Marvin Gardens," are so distinctive and individual that they are unlikely to lead directly to anyone else's work. What are the chances another essay-ist will find it appropriate to invent a tarot deck and imagine a read-ing in order to tell the story of a friendship, as Willard does? What are the odds of another essayist needing to alternate between a board game and a tour of the city it's based on, as McPhee does be-tween "Monopoly" and Atlantic City?

Other essays suggest an interplay that seems obvious enough that other writers may be prompted to experiment in their own ways with its design. For example, Wendy Rawlings opens her essay called "Vir-tually Romance: A Discourse on Love in the Information Age" with a series of epigraphs about time, the Internet, and relations between men and women and then provides a scene of a man and a woman spending time together as the consummation of an Internet rela-tionship. From that segment it braids together three strands—a series of excerpts from the couple's e-mail under the heading "Cyberspace," a series of reflections on online romance under the heading "Tempus Fugit," and a series of scenes from various states of mind in various states ("Abiding, Utah")—and concludes with sections on how to buy a personal computer and how to snorkel in the British Virgin Islands. The "crots" or segments are short, the braiding or interlocking link-age tight, and the sad and funny chronology is clear, but rather than narrate a story in chronological sequence or argue some thesis draw-ing on the example of her own experience, Rawlings experimented with form in order to discover one that would most powerfully rep-resent the reality she was writing about.

Or, to take another example, Rebecca McClanahan is similarly ex-perimental in the essay "The Riddle Song." The title refers to an old folk song which begins with a series of enigmatic statements ("I gave my love a cherry, it had no stone/I gave my love a chicken, it had no bone/I told my love a story that has no end/I gave my love a baby with no crying"), then questions those statements ("How can there be a cherry that has no stone? . . ."), and finally explains the statements

("A cherry when it's blooming, it has no stone . . ."). Except for the story ("The story of I love you, it has no end"), the statements end up being about bringing forth life. McClanahan weaves together scenes from different times in her life involving birth, death, childhood, motherhood, generations of women interacting with one another, all threaded through the lyrics to the folk song. As in countless other contemporary examples the pattern of this essay is determined by the pattern of the experience, the juxtapositions and associations and sympathetic vibrations of accumulating knowledge—as is the pattern of Christine White's essay.

WRITING AS AN EXPERIMENTAL ART

I've been stressing the uniqueness of Christine White's essay for several reasons. One reason is to demonstrate how experimental its form is. Another is to use it as an example of the problematic value of one writer's essay as a model for another writer. By "problematic" I mean that no one else should sit down to write another nonfiction rag unless ragtime is as essential to the theme and the structure of the essay as it is in White's. One of the ways we all respond to what we read is to link it to our own experiences; this is the great power of memoir and personal narrative—as memoirist Patricia Hampl says, "You give me your story, I get mine." It's good to find a text that triggers connections with what has meaning for us, but it's problematic to use the text simply as a template for recording those connections. Writers trying to link family death, celebrity death, and popular music in imitation of "Reflection Rag" are inviting disaster that isn't unique to ragtime essays—imitating "Once More to the Lake" by E. B. White or "Politics and the English Language" by George Orwell or "Living Like Weasels" by Annie Dillard can get them into the same trap. What writers need to appreciate about any of these essays is the way the form is constructed to lead the reader through the content the way the writer her- or himself understands it.

The unfolding "narrative" of "Reflection Rag" follows the arc of the author's encounters with these synchronous connections and her blossoming awareness of their significance or meaning, instead of following the chronology of events according to the dates when they occurred. In its forward progress her essay emulates the piecing together of the puzzle she talks about but it also emulates the multiple layers of the typical rag—what she calls its "syncopations, broken rhythms, and shifting accents," its "melodies and countermelodies," its "embellishments" and "grace notes." By experimenting with the content of the essay—the disparate subtopics, the varied strands or movements or motifs—she experiments with creating an appropriately reflective form, the nonfiction equivalent of the matching of lyrics and melody in an ideally composed song. I want writers to take away from a reading of "Reflection Rag" an appreciation of what experimenting with meaning and design can accomplish, the art and power of the essay. I want them to understand that an essay needn't only march relentlessly forward from beginning to end; an essay can also dance. My primary motive for stressing the uniqueness of Christine White's essay is to encourage the uniqueness of essays by other writers. There may be some rewards or pleasures in accomplishing the predictable, but a writer's real achievement comes when she or he writes an unpredictable essay, an essay only she or he could have written, an article unique to that writer.

LIVING IN AN EXPERIMENTAL WORLD

We are all accustomed by now to read the world as texts and to use the patterns of those texts to tell our stories. So, in our nonfiction, we draw upon the repetitions and patterning of quilting; the flashbacks, flashforwards, close-ups and crane shots, cross-cutting and split-screen editing of film; the multiple-voiced alternation of first person testimony and omniscient narration, stills and stock footage and dramatizations of television documentary; the framing of photography; the juxtapositions of hypertexts and anime and comic book art. Although teachers, critics, readers, and other writers seldom seem to acknowledge it, nonfictionists have been doing this for a very long time.

The world we live in is routinely, often outrageously, experimental. We come to know that world by association, juxtaposition, disjunction, intuition, experimentation, much more than we know it by logos, linearity, conjunction, formulation. By experimenting with nonfiction we aren't rejecting formulas that would have produced a more predictable result—the only predictable outcome of writing in formulas is that the writing will be formulaic. The only predictable outcome of writing experimentally is that the writer will be more engaged, committed, and challenged by the writing, and those are the qualities in the writer that most predictably generate better writing. When we experiment with nonfiction we are simply doing nonfiction the way it *needs* to be done, because nonfiction is an experimental art.

NOTES FOR NONFICTIONISTS: EXPERIMENTING

Predictably, perhaps, the only predictable way to learn an experimental art is by experimenting. One strategy I've liked is what the political columnist Tom Wicker calls "assiduous string-saving"—that is, continually jotting down notes and observations about topics of personal or professional interest and thereby creating a pool of materials from which to draw when needed. This approach intensifies the kind of associations writers often make from memory. Lists and notes and clippings build webs of associations that may be completed when the writer makes fruitful connections, perhaps inadvertently, later on. The newspaper columnist Jim Fitzgerald kept a folder of notes and clippings and often leafed through it looking for associations between seemingly disparate items to leap out at him and inspire an exploratory essay. The poet and essayist Sydney Lea often asks his students to find topics to link in two separate, perhaps not obviously related journal entries. In these instances, the writer trusts the subconscious mind to recognize associations that are in some way important or intriguing and also trusts the process of composing to lead from those premises to further discoveries. There's no formula for entering this kind of composition, and no possibility that a detached, disinterested writer will achieve anything this way. It requires ongoing engagement and the expectation that experimenting will lead to discovery. You're keeping yourself alert to possibility all the time instead of only when you've decided to write something, a particularly vital mindset if you're a regular columnist or a frequent blogger or an exploratory essayist or a freelance journalist.

Another way of experimenting with associations—and one that will often (although not inevitably) result in a segmented essay—is the creation of an exploratory grid. To do this you draw horizontal and vertical lines on a sheet of paper to form nine to twelve boxes; then by freewriting—simply allowing yourself to write what comes to you—you enter into the boxes as many associations with a chosen topic as you can think of—vignettes, anecdotes, images, literary (including musical and cinematic) allusions, family or historical parallels, and the like. Clustering and mapping exercises can have a similar effect. What are the personal, artistic, social, psychological associations you make with your topic? What kinds of evidence and reference connect to your central image or event? If the reader were invited to leap from one section of the grid to another and then to another, in what order would you arrange the items on the grid? What would you discard? What would you add? You can then look over the grid and ask yourself what boxes connect best (most powerfully, most intriguingly) for you, then pursue them into the drafting of experimental sections. This approach is like constructing a wall out of field stones, hefting them for weight and balance, pondering their shapes and determining the best way they will fit together, deciding which ones can't be used and should be set aside or discarded. One of the things writers know is that you don't always use all the sections you write. (I wrote a long segmented essay about Moraine Park in Rocky Mountain National Park and kept struggling to include a section on the roche moutonnée, a rock formation that fascinated me; eventually I had to realize that it didn't really fit the theme of my essay and that I couldn't use it. I still want to write about the roche moutonnée and have kept what I have already written, but I have accepted that, if I ever write more about it, it will go into some different essay.)

If you have any familiarity with building a website, you already have some experience with this kind of segmented exploration of a topic. Websites are made up of separate webpages connected by hyperlinks. Some of the challenges of composing the website are determining where and when to start new pages, how they're interlinked, what you want to do about influencing the order in which the online reader visits the various pages, and what the consequences might be of reading them in a random order. Print texts, of course, are always fundamentally linear—read from left to right, top to bottom, first page to last in our culture—no matter how "disjunctive" or "segmented" they may be, but the segmented essay and the website have a lot in common. If the cells of your grid were pages of your website, which would be the homepage, what hyperlinks would you attach to it, and where would the links take the reader?

Yet another approach, even more visually oriented than these first two, is to think about the parts of your topic as an arrangement of images. As you'll see in the next chapter, I use photographs as heuristic (discovery) devices a great deal in my own writing and have carried the habit over into classes and workshops. I think of a unified, conjunctive essay as like a single photograph—for example, the World War II photograph by Robert Capa of two American soldiers, a young Italian woman, and an elderly Italian bootblack gathered around a shoeshine stand in Palermo; I think of a segmented, disjunctive essay as like a medieval altarpiece—for example, Jan van Eyck's Adoration of the Lamb (Ghent) Altarpiece, a polyptych of multiple panels depicting the Last Judgment, the earthly paradise with worshipful saints, and the figures of Adam and Eve. The Capa is the kind of photograph we're most accustomed to, one unified image recording a single moment in a single scene; the van Eyck, divided into separate panels juxtaposing single figures with landscapes and group portraits and differences of scale and emphasis, demands an associative, cumulative reading. A while ago I copied both images onto my computer and with the help of a photo-editing program I was able to remove images from the frames around panels of the van Eyck altarpiece and substitute in some of those now-empty frames images from the Capa photograph. Immediately such a visual arrangement suggests to an observer that there is more than one way to represent the event, more than one level of meaning that can be depicted in the images. It is interesting to imagine what images might be found to fill the blank panels in the "Capa polyptych"; the selections would depend upon who the person supplying the images is and how he or she relates to the images already provided—if the Sicilian scene represents what might be seen by a reporter or researcher, the panels would be filled with something different than what would be placed there by someone seeing it as a participant or as a descendant of any of the people in the scene or as an individual who has lived a similar scene. The images in the panels are equivalent to segments in an essay; when we realize that, then we are ready to begin experimenting with an essay as we have experimented with the multi-paneled altarpiece, substituting prose for pictures.

Some essays are snapshots, candid pictures; some are studio portraits, formal and posed; some are polyptychs, arrangements of various images that create a collective, multi-faceted whole. Before you can experiment with form, you need to have an awareness of how flexible the form of nonfiction can be.

4

THE ART OF SEEING

I

"The art of seeing in nonfiction" is not simply a metaphor for perception or understanding in writing, it's also an interpretive visual act. Not only can we better understand what we're doing in nonfiction by approaching it in terms of "reading" images, we also can actually draw on images as a way of comprehending our subject or our response to it. Even if we've never seen a particular picture before, we still tend to read it for information and still go beyond information into interpretation, just as we do with events in our lives.

For example, in that photograph by Robert Capa mentioned in the last chapter, four people gather around a shoeshine stand. On the viewer's right a young bareheaded man with a Red Cross armband sits on the stand and smiles at the camera while an elderly man at his feet, bottom left, turns his head in the direction of two other people near the stand; at the center of the picture a slender, neatly dressed young woman stands close to a helmeted soldier who has his right arm around her, his fingers barely visible emerging on her right shoulder. She looks up at him with a tight-lipped smile; he looks down at her with a grin and a gaze that doesn't meet her eyes but seems directed at her mouth or neck. The black-and-white photo, the uniforms on the younger men, the fashion of the woman's hair and dress, the snatches of Italian words in the background, the architecture, the *lustrascarpe*'s shoeshine stand—all these things help identify the scene as somewhere in Italy during World War II.

I am trying to give a fairly flat, objective description of the photo, the kind of initial reading people volunteer when I have displayed it and asked for clarification of its contents, but it's relatively difficult not to veer into interpretation. Viewers draw on information stored in memory to sort out this much of the identification of the photo, and their accuracy may depend on their age, their experience, their reading, their encounters with similar photos, their philosophy or politics. Some people who see the picture read the original caption, "Palermo, Sicily. July 1943. Americans enjoying victory," without irony. They feel a sense of relief that some American fighting men are being met cordially by some of the Sicilians they liberated from Axis control. Other people view the scene somewhat smirkingly, noting the gazes the woman and the helmeted soldier are giving one another and anticipating the spoils that may accompany this victory. Still others are disturbed by the picture, the seemingly thoughtless grin of the corpsman in the chair and the proprietary grip of the helmeted soldier on the woman, whose stiffness belies her smile but seems to make the *lustrascarpe* tense. When I look at the picture I remember later photos in the same book (Capa's memoir, *Slightly Out of Focus*) that show French women whose children were fathered by German soldiers, their heads shaved, a jeering throng hounding them down the streets of Chartres, demeaned and degraded for collaborating with foreign troops. The juxtaposition colors my reading of the Palermo photo. I try to see that picture as the Americans in the photo might see it, as the woman might see it, as the *lustrascarpe* might see it; I wonder how the children of any of the people in the photo might see it years later; I try to see it as the "liberated" peoples of Afghanistan or Iraq or Panama might see it. If any of them were to write a caption for this photo, would it read like the one that was originally published with it?

Or consider the famous picture by Joe Rosenthal of Marines raising the American flag on Mt. Suribachi during the World War II battle for Iwo Jima. It is a picture so vivid and moving that it has been reproduced countless times—on stamps, posters, magazine covers, the U.S. Marine Memorial sculpture—as representative of heroism under fire, the indefatigable spirit of the American fighting man, the selfless teamwork of men in battle, the essence of what it means to be a Marine. Relatively few people, except for the men in the picture, now all dead, and the man who took it and the readers of James Bradley's book *Flags of Our Fathers* know most of the key facts about the photo: that the picture was taken almost accidentally; that it was the second flag raising on that spot, done to replace the original, smaller flag; that at the moment the flag was raised Mt. Suribachi was safe enough that no one involved thought of the act as risky, as anything other than a momentary chore; that three of the six men were killed in battle over the next few days. It is a great, evocative, stirring photograph, but what we see in it is influenced not only by what we read into body language and visual elements but also by how much we know and how we situate the photo in its context. According to James Bradley, whose father, a Navy corpsman, not a Marine, is the man in profile in the picture, the three survivors—John Bradley, Ira Hayes, and Rene Gagnon—and Joe Rosenthal, the photographer, saw the picture differently than the *Life* editor in New York who cropped and published it and differently than the American public who reacted only to the cropped image in print. The art of seeing also depends on what we bring to the viewing and where we get that information.

Or consider the well-known photograph by Dorothea Lange called "Migrant Mother." It is one of the great iconic American photographs, seeming to encapsulate an era and to individualize the experience of millions in the Dust Bowl and the Depression. It also seems to embody, in the look on her face and the sheltered weight of the children upon her, something about careworn but resilient motherhood. Any number of people writing about what they see in this photo would produce a range of responses—subjective-personal, cultural-critical, aesthetic-interpretive, objective-expository. As Robert Coles writes in

Doing Documentary Work, his book exploring the recording and interpretation of reality through photographs, "Who we are . . . determines
what we notice and . . . what we regard as worthy of notice, what we
find significant." Everything's a Rorschach test. Lange's picture can be
discussed as photography, art, photojournalism, history, sociology,
psychology, rhetoric, aesthetics, women's studies, environmental studies, fashion, architecture, biology, health, and more. It is also evidence
for autobiography and memoir. In 1983, at seventy-nine, Florence
Thompson, the woman in the picture, died of cancer. Nine of her ten
children were still living when she died. Perhaps one of them—one of
the children in the picture—or a grandchild or great-grandchild will
write a unique caption for the photo or an essay about personal history, not about iconic photography.

Nonfiction is the written expression of, reflection upon, or interpretation of observed, perceived, or recollected experience. Expression, reflection, and interpretation are determined by whether the
eye of the beholder belongs to a spectator or a participant. Whether
the result is confession, testimony, reportage, or analysis, it begins
with the art of seeing.

II

This is a visual age. Texts, literary or otherwise, have always been a
means of transferring the images in a writer's mind into a reader's
mind. Some scholars have argued that we think in images; when we
write, we are attempting to find words that will accurately represent
those images both to ourselves and also to others, and when we read
we are attempting to translate our own or someone else's words back
into images. If this is so, then in our media-driven age, with its attention to the visual, images are made problematic by their ability to
bypass the intermediary stages of language—the communication is
expressed directly in images and the viewer receives them directly,
intuitively, without the need for interaction and translation. Such a
circumstance makes it important that we all learn how to "read" im-

ages, to understand visual rhetoric, because images are simultaneously both medium and message.

Trying to help writers become better readers of images as well as use images as resources for writing, I've devised an activity I call "captioning." I ask people to draw upon images stored in their minds, stuffed in their billfolds, tacked on their bulletin boards, and use them to trigger memory, develop description, and spark reflection. They can capture the past by captioning the images that open windows into the past for them. The visual is one of the thresholds we can cross to enter all forms of nonfiction, especially—but not exclusively—memoir.

My term for this strategy was inspired by a feature in *Civilization*, the now-defunct magazine of the Library of Congress. A department titled "Caption" and subtitled "What's in a Picture?" was written by a different writer in each issue; it was a single page with a photograph (or sometimes an art object) accompanied by a writer's response to or interpretation of the picture. For example, Mark O'Donnell's caption remarked on cloning in the context of a photograph of him and his twin brother; Francine Prose gave a close reading of a wry, quirky self-portrait taken by the nineteenth-century photographer Frances Benjamin. The photos on the "Caption" page ranged from the personal to the journalistic to the artistic, from snapshots to documentary footage to art photography.

One of the approaches a writer can take to a photograph is to read it from a personal perspective. On her contribution to the "Captions" page, the novelist Carol Shields, who grew up in Winnipeg, Manitoba, displays a picture of an unidentified woman that she found in her mother's photo album. The solid, mature figure stands on a set of side porch steps against a snowy background. By close reading of the image Shields gleans a great deal of information about the context for the picture.

The scene speaks to me strongly of Winnipeg: the limestone foundation of the house, the board siding and the bright prairie sunlight breaking through the bare branches. It must be a relatively mild day in late October or November, since the awning has not yet been taken down for the winter. Any moment now this awning will be weighed down with snow or torn to shreds by the ferocious winds that sweep in from the north. Manitoba is a place of climate extremes, with one season usurping the other, and without warning.

The woman's face and body strike me as a brilliant mixture of vulnerability and strength. That sprightly hat, those thickly stockinged legs, that practical coat belted against the cold! The softness in her face is countered by a certain tension in the arms and the way in which her hands are clutched and drawn into her sleeves for warmth.

Shields deduces a great deal about this woman from the details in the picture, concluding that she must be a widow "for otherwise those snowy steps would have been shoveled clean" but also that she "doesn't look like a hibernator." For Shields, this is not simply a photograph of an older woman on porch steps in winter but an occasion for drawing on her own experience of Manitoba living. As Robert Coles explains in *Doing Documentary Work*, "Each of us brings, finally, a particular life to the others being observed in documentary work, and so to some degree, each of us will engage with those others differently, carrying back from such engagement our own version of them." Nonfiction sets us in touch with who we are and where we come from even in an ostensibly simple act of description like this.

Another example of captioning, Geoff Dyer's response to Robert Capa's photograph titled "Italian Soldier After End of Fighting, Sicily, 1943," gives an imaginative response evoked by an historical image. The picture shows an Italian soldier walking down a dirt road next to a woman with a bicycle. For Dyer, the photograph "shows the moment when all the unvoiced hopes . . . of all lovers separated by war" come true. This is how he describes the picture:

The hot Mediterranean landscape. Dust on the bicycle tires. Sun on her tanned arms. Their shadows mingling. The sizzle of cicadas, the slow whir of the bicycle. The photograph would be diminished without that bicycle; it would be ruined without her long hair. Her hair tells us: This is how she was when he left; she has not changed; she has remained true to him.

She asks about the things that have happened to him; he is hesitant at first, but there is no hurry. Eventually, he tells her of the friends he has lost, the terrible things he has seen. He is impatient for news of friends and relatives back in their village. She tells about her brother who was also in the army, about the funny thing that happened with the schoolteacher and the butcher's dog.

Dyer's caption essay, like Shields's, pushes the viewer's response toward the picture into the borderland between nonfiction and fiction; his is more of an imaginative explanation inspired by a historical photograph, like a poem about a painting, and hers is closer to the immediate experience of herself and her family, but both are reading the evidence of images from other lives.

Joyce Carol Oates, however, uses a very personal image to conjure a very personal past. It was the first "Caption" page I ever read and it was a serendipitous discovery, since it appeared when I was working on a family memoir set in the same town outside of which Oates herself grew up. She explains the context for the snapshot of her mother and herself taken on May 14, 1941 this way:

> My 27-year-old father, Frederic Oates, "Freddy," taking snapshots of my mother and me on this sunny afternoon, is worried about being drafted into the army; in the meantime he's working at Harrison Radiator, a division of General Motors in Lockport, New York, involved in what is unofficially believed to be "defense work" (airplanes). It's a tense, unpredictable era in our history, yet such global turbulence is remote from the grassy backyard of our family home in Millersport, New York; here is a leafy, spacious world, in which my 24-year-old mother, Carolina, and I, an inquisitive child of three years 11 months, appear to be playing with new-born kittens. How happy we must have seemed to that long-lost "Joyce Carol," with little more vexing in her life than the ordeal of having curly hair combed free of snarls and prettily fixed with a ribbon, and being "dressed up" for some adult special occasion.

She notes the black-barked cherry tree, the frame house of her grandparents, the outside cellar door, the rain barrel. The photograph is a way back into the past, a way of locating herself, giving herself a position from which to speculate and reflect about family, history, personal experience. At the end of this half-page article she writes:

> Memory is our domestic form of time travel. The invention of photography—in particular, the "snapshot"—revolutionized human consciousness, for when we claim to "remember" our pasts, we are surely remembering our favorite snapshots, in which the long-faded past is given a distinct visual immortality. Just as art provides answers long before we understand the questions, so, too, our relationship with our distant past, in particular our relationship with our parents, is a phenomenon we come to realize only by degrees, as we too age, across the mysterious abyss of time.

If Oates is right, that "when we claim to 'remember' our pasts, we are surely remembering our favorite snapshots," then those images can serve to bridge that abyss of time and help us capture the past.

This is an insight memoirists have been drawing on all along. In *All but the Waltz*, a memoir by Mary Clearman Blew, the chapters are all preceded by family photographs which serve as direct or indirect sources of inspiration. The section titled "Reading Abraham" begins, "As far back as I can remember, a framed photograph of my great-grandparents hung in the house where I grew up." Blew recounts her search through her great-grandfather's papers in an effort to bring him to life and returns to the portrait of Abraham and Mary toward chapter's end, where she writes:

> Abraham, your photograph hangs over my desk. Above the reflection on the glass from the window opposite, Mary stands stalwart behind you while your gaze is set eternally over my shoulder. In the reflection, superimposed over you and Mary in your good formal dark clothes, the Snake River spreads its current as it rolls toward its confluence. The early lights of winter glow on the far bank of the Snake and glow again in the reflected depths of your photograph. I am a long way from home.

Photographs are not always such overt presences in the chapters of this book, but they are often implicit support for detail and tone and supplement the prose.

Bret Lott similarly includes a small snapshot of the principle characters at the beginning of each interlinked essay of his memoir, *Fathers, Sons, and Brothers,* and a folding wallet of cellophane-encased photos spills down the dust jacket of the book. In one chapter, "Brothers," the opening segment describes a brief scene from a home movie from 1960, around a California swimming pool, in which his brother Brad, then four, pinches the author, then a year and a half; the second segment describes a snapshot of the brothers from 1980, their arms around each other. The remainder of the essay accounts for the gap in between photos and compares the brothers to the author's two sons. In the final segment of the essay Lott writes:

> I have no memory of the pinch Brad gave me on the edge of that apartment-complex pool, no memory of my mother's black hair—now it's a sort of brown—nor even any memory of the pool itself. There is only that bit of film.
>
> But I can remember putting my arm around his shoulder in 1980, leaning into him, the awkward and alien comfort of that touch. . . .
>
> What I believe is this: That pinch was entry into our childhood; my arm around him, our smiling, is the proof of us two surfacing, alive but not unscathed.
>
> And here are my own two boys, already embarked.

Because the photographs that accompany the essays are so apt, and because they sometimes turn up, as here, central to the content of an essay, we can see here the aptness of Oates's remark that our memories of events are often memories of photographs of events.

In fact, Simone Poirier-Bures opens her memoir of Crete, *That Shining Place,* with a description of a photograph. "In the photo I remember, Maria looks straight at the camera," she begins, and then describes Maria and her children in detail, observing of the oldest son that he "stands a little apart from the others, as if, as the only male, he feels a need to disassociate himself from the women." She describes the expression on their faces and the yellowish-brown peeling stucco wall behind them. "I remember also in this picture the hindquarters of a donkey, a brown shaggy one who carried things for the old man who delivered goods to the small store a few doors down, but perhaps I am confusing this photo with another." The uncertainty about whether a part of the donkey is in the picture is followed by a description of individuals not in the portrait, the husband who is always absent, the *Yaya*, or grandmother, who is always behind the scenes. Only later, in the afterword to the book, does the author admit that, when she found the actual photograph she had been thinking of, the descriptions she had written didn't match the actual expressions and attitudes of the people she described; that was the point where she added the phrase, "I remember," because the memory of the photograph was more important than the photograph itself.

These examples suggest how useful, even how vital, photographs or the memories of photographs often are to a writer's accessing of memory for an essay or a memoir. Taking these hints I began working a family memoir of my own, shifting through snapshots to see where they would lead me, what they would connect me to. The work has led so far to at least one essay where every segment enters personal history through the windows of photographs. The book-length memoir that (I hope) will follow is so dependent on responses to photographs as jumping off places for essays that I subtitled the work-in-progress *An Album*.

III

One way a writer can understand the art of seeing is to spontaneously write about a couple of photographs—freewrite, I mean, for several minutes, simply responding to the images before her. If one of the photos is her own, a picture of family or friends, and another is unfamiliar, a photo by or about someone else, so much the better. There's something to be learned by writing in the first place and more to be learned about writing about both something familiar and something unfamiliar.

This is what the writer learns: When she tries to describe what she sees in a photograph she carries with her or keeps on her dresser or desk, she soon begins to *explain* the context for the picture, the identity of the person or persons in it, the reason she carries or displays this photo, its significance to her. When she tries to describe what she sees in someone else's photograph, particularly the photograph carried by a stranger, she soon begins to *interpret* context, identity, background, and significance. If she were to compare her explanation or her interpretation with those of another writer who had written about the same two pictures, she would find certain descriptive common ground but also, depending on the nature of the picture, a considerable divergence of comprehension and response. The meaning of the picture changes with the eye of the beholder, particularly when the beholder sees with the eye of the participant or the eye of the spectator. The art of seeing depends upon perception, observation, close attention, but also upon the identity of the viewer.

Here's an example of what I mean: A student once showed me a photograph of three men kneeling over the bodies of three dead deer, lifting the heads by the antlers and smiling into the camera. It was night and the ground was snow-covered and the photographer used a flash to illuminate the scene. The figure in the center was the student, then about seventeen, clean-shaven, rosy-cheeked. On his right was a man in his late thirties, with unkempt dark hair and moustache and a day-old beard and a haggard smile; on his left was an older man, in his fifties perhaps, his hair and moustache mostly gray, his face more puffy and grizzled, his smile gap-toothed. Clearly the unshaven men were related, though it was less obvious that the man in the middle was son and grandson to the others.

I have tried to be "objective" here, merely descriptive of the picture's composition, but I slip easily into interpretation. This is a commemorative photo of a successful deer hunt for three generations of hunters—that much is clear. Were I to use it as a starting point for an essay of mine, I would comment on the sense of family tradition I see, the likelihood that this family has yearly hunted deer for as long as anyone can remember, the camaraderie that exists here, the sense of community, the bonds of violence and conquest. Since I do not hunt and do not sympathize much with killing, I might ruminate some on the ways children adopt the mores of their elders, might editorialize about alternative ways of creating the bonds among males that seem so central to this picture.

My student has a different reading of the picture. To him it is an anomaly. "It seems so unlikely that the three of us should be seen together with smiles on our faces," he writes. His grandfather, a former Marine who survived the sinking of his vessel in World War II, "sat in the bar spending the money needed to raise his family of nine" while his wife raised the children. His father, who at seventeen survived a car wreck that killed his four best friends, was in jail when the author was born; "I too saw little of my father in my childhood years as he bounced back and forth between jail and home." Three days after the photograph was taken, father and son had a tremendous argument that ended when the son moved out of the family house. He writes, "That's why this picture is so memorable for me. What would bring the three of us together this day with smiles on our faces? From the picture, nobody can see these differences between us. You only see a son, his father, and his father's father happily showing off the deer they bagged on this beautiful November night." He keeps the picture around because it shows absolutely nothing of the reality of his life.

Once the student explained the picture from his perspective, I read the photo differently than I originally had. But when *I* write about it now, I write about the way I behold that student beholding that photograph. I can never write the story he can write. The art of seeing has to include the angle at which the viewer beholds the object of his or her vision.

IV

The "Caption" pages of *Civilization* fascinated me. I pondered the possibilities personal images might offer writers, myself included, in their attempts to capture the past. Eventually, thinking about using such a form in classrooms and workshops, I experimented on myself with a long journal entry that I hoped would model the kind of writing I was looking for. Leafing through family pictures I found two photographs taken circa 1952 in Cooperstown, New York, around the statue of James Fenimore Cooper, and simply wrote an impromptu response to them. At the time I was teaching in a computer class-room and, because our word-processing program was equipped to add photographs in texts, I scanned in the photos and, after I had completed the journal entry on the computer, I inserted the photos into the document.

My Cooperstown journal and the "Caption" pages I've mentioned illustrate the possibilities of writing what I think of as "caption essays." If we attempt close description of what we see in a photograph, we find that it surfaces context, meaning, and perspective. For example, in my Cooperstown journal, I thought I detected differences in photographers from evidence in the two pictures. In the picture of my mother, sister, brother, cousin, and me, the photographer must have been my father, who lay on the grass to get the shot and made the statue behind us the center of the shot. In the picture of only us children, the photographer seems to have been my mother, who centered on the children, not the statue.

Distance in time from the moment of the photo provides the opportunity for reflection. In the Cooperstown journal, written some forty years after the event, I knew what had happened to those people in the picture, I knew the context of their lives when the picture was taken, and I found myself wondering whether photographs can be trusted at all as a record of any other than physical location in time.

A journal entry centered on captioning allows a writer to explore photos in his or her own way. I invited students to use the captioning journal as the basis for a personal essay, but, because these subjects often are very personal, I left it up to them whether they pursued that topic or chose another. The essential element of my teaching, as well as an important element of my own composing, has been to continually attempt to get the writer working subconsciously on writing, to find different ways to set synapses firing that involuntarily open the way to topic and memory and attitude. So I would ask students to bring one or two photographs to class and I projected some of them offered by volunteers up on a screen at the front of the room for the rest of us to "read"—that is, to describe and interpret. Students would write a log entry on the photographs as a way of reacting spontaneously to the photos, and then the captioning journal entry invited them to develop their interpretations and reactions.

If writers are asked to think of one photo they might write about or one photo that most powerfully comes to mind when someone proposes this idea, they usually settle on one or two very quickly. Often, even in the first burst of identifying the photos, they begin to get at the underlying context of such pictures for them. Some examples of first thoughts:

When I think about photographs, I automatically get visual images of the photos from my childhood. They define much of what I am today. The tomboy of the neighborhood who was always considered one of the guys.

I begin to think about the picture around my neck. . . . It is a picture of me, my mom, and my dad. They got married just before I was born. And they divorced when I was no more than three.

I immediately think of the pictures I can go back to the dorm and get right now if you asked.

When I think of this assignment I already have my picture picked out. The picture I brought in was a picture I took of my friends one night while we were out mudding. We had finally conquered a hole that we were looking at for days. Everyone was so happy that I decided to take a picture. I made sure that the smoke from the jeep was in the picture to show people that we actually made it through the hole.

I brought the six pictures that always stay in my Day Planner. However, the main picture is of my husband (then boyfriend) and me at prom. We are 18 years old and not really happy. We are both uncomfortable because we are dressed up.

It is a picture from my childhood. I was probably about three, maybe four. I am lying in my pajamas fast asleep in a dresser drawer. I used to sleep there as a younger child.

Often the photographs people choose are ones that they identify with the best times with friends or family or those that picture friends and family they've lost. Perhaps photographs are not only a way to get in touch with the past but also a way to recognize the losses we've suffered, often incrementally or inadvertently, over time.

Take the child sleeping in the drawer, for example. In her captioning journal entry Kelli gives the date of the picture as February 1983, when she was "a month shy of age three." She writes, "I am wearing floral printed pajamas. These pajamas were most likely created by my grandmother, like many of my childhood clothes were. The dresser I am sleeping in was made from Grandfather's own crafty hands." These are good details, which I think emerge from trying to write about what she sees. They aren't part of the earlier log entry, which is acceptably vague and brief. In the journal entry she writes, "I am huddled up in the fetal position cuddling with my favorite blanket." She remembers that she called the blanket her Binky and that she was eight or nine before her mother made her give it up. Then her description of herself surfaces the underlying reason this picture has meaning for her.

> I am in a peaceful slumber. I am in my own childlike cocoon. Sometimes I wish I could go back to my childlike cocoon. My mother once told me that on that day she had thought she lost me. She searched the whole house up and down screaming my name aloud. I of course had blocked out the confusion around me. Now I realize it's time for me to wake up from my cocoon and face the confusion head on.

In the remainder of the journal entry she talks about trying to "slowly and carefully break away from the shelters my parents have put around me," how she rose above the barriers in adolescence and was gently guided back to shelter. She concludes, "I am beginning to wake from peaceful slumber and realize it's time to grow up and face reality. It's time for me to give up the cozy comfort of 'Binky' and break away from the enclosing shelter of the drawer." As a college freshman living away from home, she is using her analysis of this photograph to get at both why she treasures the picture and how it connects to deep-seated and important issues for her, about separation, about independence, about the difference between being nurtured and being constrained.

Another writer chose to write about a photograph of her daughter Kelcey and another little girl named Alexis, both six-year-old flower girls at a family wedding. After describing the circumstances and the costumes, Brenda begins to reflect on the picture.

> The pose touches me, their arms about each other, having forged a bond of friendship through participating in a ritual they did not fully understand or particularly enjoy. Their disheveled dresses and bare feet bespeak the whimsy of children to put off pomp and pretense in favor of dancing themselves into exhaustion for the sheer joy of it.

And then Brenda gets beyond the moment and deeper into the significance of the photograph for her:

> Seeing her dressed up was a portent of moments to come between my daughter and me. Hazy scenes of dates, dances, proms, and shadows of her own wedding flickered in my mind. I was aware as I took this picture that others like it were to come in our lives together. The events and rituals of a daughter growing, maturing, coming of age and beginning her own independent life are timeless and inescapable in some form or another.

This is the other side of Kelli's captioning journal, by a mother instead of a daughter.

Writers often reach such insights by the end of their journal entries. The photographs give them a focus for reflection, perhaps make it easier to be aware of their emotions at particular moments, to recall them and, better yet, to respond to them. One student wrote about a picture of her aged grandfather with a stack of Christmas presents on his lap. When she compares that picture to those of him at other Christmases, she realizes that although his pose and his slight smile are similar to those of the past, this photo records something different. Her grandfather is in advanced stages of Alzheimer's. "My grandpa is holding all his unwrapped packages because this year he does not know how to open them," she writes, and then she realizes that the picture captures a pose he sat in virtually unchanging throughout the day. She asks, "Yes, my grandpa is in the picture—but is that really him anymore?" It's a painful and perplexing question.

Not all the writing that this captioning opportunity produces is as intense or insightful as some of these examples are. But the journal entries often help the writers get more deeply into subject matter. For example, one person who began with a description of a photograph of her soccer teammates and herself on a gondola in Venice recalled that this was the first picture of that gondola ride, and it led her to write a brief travel essay recreating the voyage through the canals.

The pictures also help writers avoid the wheel spinning or throat clearing that often takes up early pages of an early draft. Instead they often seem to plunge into the heart of the subject, as these opening lines demonstrate:

> It would be one of the last times the three of us would be together, Karin, Robin, and I.

> I had not seen her for a few years when I received this picture of her.

> I always keep it around my neck. I never realized what it really meant. . . . Until I looked at it I didn't understand that it seemed to be the beginning of a mistake.

These openings are immediate and direct and seem to be inspired by an eagerness to engage the photographs rather than stand back and point out their features from a distance. From these beginnings they go deeper into the subject, but the images themselves have made going deeper possible sooner than writing about the same moment or person or event without the impetus from images would have done.

Exploring the photograph seems to be a highly charged method of getting back into memory and connecting to all the elements of the experience more directly. It's as if you don't simply remain a spectator of the photograph but are able somehow to enter it, to reinhabit the moment it documents, to wander through it, turn around, and look back out at yourself as viewer, the part of your self that needs to record what the part of the self in the photo observes or discovers. Once you're able to do that, it may be easier to do the same thing with the images you only recall or imagine, the ones not reinforced by photographs but nonetheless slipped into the album of memory.

This "captioning" process in a journal entry, then, is part of the nonfictionist's arsenal of discovery strategies. If it only brings us closer to interpretation or memory, it's done all we can hope for in journalkeeping, but sometimes it brings us far enough that it becomes a draft of an essay or a section of a memoir or a more confident part of reportage. By captioning the images of our lives or our experiences or even our research, we are also developing strategies that will help us capture—and write—the past. That's what's valuable about cultivating the art of seeing in nonfiction.

NOTES FOR NONFICTIONISTS: SEEING

The art of seeing is something that practice improves. Nature writers know that, in John Burroughs's term, keeping "a sharp lookout" is the best way to develop the knack for observing the natural world. Haste and preoccupation divert our attention from what's right in front of us; slowing down and concentrating can make what seems invisible or nonexistent appear before us in great detail. For the nature writer and the travel writer, that means being alert and observant right where they are; for the rest of us it might come about through images. The writing activities that follow might simply heighten your powers of observation, but they might also lead you into topics worthy of further development.

Let's focus on that captioning idea, using your journal or writing log or simply a 5 × 8 note card as a place to write about what you see or think you see. To begin with, think of a photograph that has particular significance for you, perhaps one you hold dear or at least think you know well. Without looking at it, spend a few minutes describing everything you remember seeing in the photo. Try to be objective in your description, as if you were writing for someone unfamiliar with the photo or with its contents, someone who has to visualize it from your description. By this I mean, describe it as if you didn't know when or where it was taken or who was in the picture, but were simply itemizing its elements—not "our family reunion at Aunt Mary's in July 1983" but "a group of people of varying ages getting food from one table on a sunshiny, summery day"; not "Uncle Al" but "a round-faced man roughly fifty to sixty years old, wearing a John Deere cap and a denim work shirt, sleeves rolled up revealing tanned, muscular forearms and heavy, thick hands, broad-shouldered but also heavy in the stomach, a button missing from the middle of his shirt front." Write for ten or fifteen minutes. Be sure to indicate not only who, where, and when but also what the setting is like and how people are behaving.

Then track down the original photograph and compare your memory of it to the reality of the image. How well did you remember it? What facts need correcting? What interpretation needs adjusting? What accounts for the way you read the picture in memory and the way you read it when it's physically before you? Now write about the differences in the details and also about your reactions to what you see and what you thought you saw. Consider what the comparison says about your feelings about the picture.

The results of such an exercise aren't completely predictable, but, depending on the nature of the photo and the degree of discrepancy between your description and your viewing, it may tell you something about yourself—not just your feelings about the picture but your feelings about the subject or the circumstance or the background context of the picture. This is what, in different ways, happened to Simone Poirier-Bures with her photo from Crete and Terry Tempest Williams with the Bosch triptych.

This doesn't have to be an activity drawn only from photos; it could be an exercise in testing and strengthening the images you carry with you in memory or even experience in the moment. Try this right now: Open your notebook, put it in a position where you can write on it and, WITHOUT LOOKING UP FROM THIS PAGE OR FROM THE NOTEBOOK, write a detailed description of the location where you're reading or writing. What's there? Who's there? How's it decorated or landscaped? Write for ten or fifteen minutes. Then look up and compare your description with your actual locale. Again deal with facts and interpretation. Account for what you've ignored or overlooked. (You can also do this for a location you *aren't* in at the moment but think you know well. Write your description, then go there and compare your writing with the actual locale.)

What I think you will discover in these experiments is that whatever is seen is determined by the eye of the beholder. Who you are determines what you pay attention to. As a nonfictionist, you need to be not only an accurate observer but also one who is both aware of how she sees things and willing to crosscheck the reliability of what she thinks she sees—in pictures, in the actual scene, and in memory. Not incidentally, what you do in these experiments is the kind of thing you may have to do with writing in progress—verify your account of things by consulting photographs (or other research materials) or by returning to the actual scene or setting to make certain you have it right.

Another way of approaching images is the one discussed in this chapter, investigating a particular image as a way to enter the past. Either as an experiment or as a prewriting occasion for a topic you've been planning to write about, find an image that relates to the topic—for a family story it might be a group photo of family members in a relevant setting; for a travel narrative it might be a postcard of a place you've been to; for a review or a piece of reportage it might be an on-the-spot photo. Begin by describing in detail what you see in the image, but also try to go a little further by imagining or recalling yourself in the setting of the image. Close your eyes, step into the image, and walk around, noting what you see. Then open your eyes and record what you noticed as you "virtually" walked around inside the image. Be specific in details but don't neglect your feelings, whatever emotions surface; just make certain you explain what provoked those feelings.

This kind of activity can do several things: it can surface physical and psychological details; it can make the moment seem more immediate and present rather than distant and past; it can serve as a draft for a section of a work-in-progress; it can open you up to the reasons the topic matters to you. Perhaps what you write goes into the piece as a description of a photo, or perhaps it goes into the piece as a fully recovered or realized scene, or perhaps it provokes other, more significant memories or scenes and serves only as a freewrite that moves you forward and never leaves your journal in any form. The important thing is that it engages you more fully with what you see.

All of this has been drawing on images as resource. It's also possible to use images another way to generate material for a writing project. This approach reverses what we've been talking about. Instead of using an image to re-create an experience, you can use an experience to create an image. Let's say you had something about your first formal date or a particular event in your work experience that you thought you could write about but were having difficulty getting all the details organized. Imagine seeing that event through the eyes of a photographer, as images selected and preserved on your camera's memory card or in a folder of snapshots or as a brief slide show. If you could have only half a dozen pictures of the event, how would you arrange the shots so that they captured what, in your mind, was the essence of the experience? "There are no pictures of the event but if I had been the photographer recording it, here are the shots I would have taken" could be your opening sentence. Following through on this will anchor the highlights of the event in your mind and perhaps capture pertinent but overlooked or nearly forgotten details you can use as the composing progresses.

Images make us search for appropriate words; words make us envision particular images. In nonfiction we continually wrestle with the difficulty of making words and images connect to one another in the most reliable, accurate way. That's what makes the art of seeing so important in nonfiction.

5

COLLAGE, MONTAGE, MOSAIC, VIGNETTE, EPISODE, SEGMENT

It's a common problem among novice writers, starting too far back in the narrative or trying to encompass too much time or too much activity in a single chronology. A narrative about high school begins at the moment the writer entered the building for the first time in ninth grade and moves inexorably toward the moment of graduation, growing more perfunctory year by year; a story about making the team or the cheerleading squad presents a minute-by-minute account of decision, preparation, and competition that loses more and more energy the longer it goes on.

But it isn't only a novice writer's problem. Any writer runs up against the insidious demands of linear presentation of material whenever he or she selects chronology—from the beginning to the end, from the first step through each individual step to the final step, from the inception through the planning and execution to the result—as the organizing principle of an essay or article. Linear schemes of organization come easily to us. We all tell stories and chronology is the simplest system of organization ("We began by . . . , then we . . . , and finally we . . ."); process is the most accessible scheme of exposition ("First you . . . , next you . . . , and you conclude by . . ."); linear movement structures description the most directly ("Her hair was the color . . . her feet spilling out of tattered sandals"; "On the east side of the building . . . in the middle was . . . on the west side we saw . . ."). But linear schemes don't automatically help with issues of compression and focus, particularly in an age of increasingly shorter attention spans and little patience for leisurely development of plot and character and theme.

The more complex the story is—that is, the more interwoven with other subjects, ideas, incidents, experiences it is—the harder it is to make it all connect in a linear way that doesn't extend the narrative or the development beyond the patience of writer and reader alike. Moreover, the connections and associations that come so readily in the memory and in the imagination often defy simple linearity, easy transition from one subtopic to the next, when the writer has to force them into words on a page.

Mike has been cleaning his mental attic for the past several years, rummaging through his souvenirs and writing essays about a lifetime playing sports—the high school pitching, the conflicts with coaches, the visits to historic ballparks. Now he begins an essay about how he came to give up his annual summer stint as manager and player for a fast-pitch softball team.

He starts an early draft with a brief scene set in the present that serves as the trigger for a flashback that gives him the opportunity to review his long career with the team. "It's a lazy summer evening and I'm driving home from campus," he begins, and then tells how his weariness momentarily vanishes when he notices a game in progress at the ball park where he used to play: "For a moment I want to jump out of the car, climb into my softball uniform, and trot out to my old position in left field." He recounts how he gazed longingly at the field and then reluctantly continued home. After these two brief paragraphs of introduction, in the third paragraph he makes a transition to the past: "That night, while reading, my mind wanders, and for a suspended moment it is 1969 again. That summer, I was . . ." From here he relies on the act of composing itself to help him rediscover the subject matter. Chronology decides the order. He traces the arc of his involvement from the moment he decided to join the softball team, and one memory provokes another until he reaches his last game and the end of the draft.

By then he has covered a lot of ground. His draft surfaces deep-seated feelings about playing ball, about giving it up, about the satisfactions of moving on to new places in his life and expending his energies elsewhere. But it takes a long time to get to the place where these important and powerful feelings get voiced, because so much detail has emerged in his review of the chronology—early days on the team, the change from player to manager, road trips, destinations, the interaction with players, the near-misses for spots in regional and state tournaments, the interests that distracted him from the game, the aging processes that slowed him down. In the associative links of memory every detail makes sense, makes connections, but on the page the slow linear march of the chronology dissipates all the emphatic force of the narrative—there's a reason no one tried to cash in on the natural disaster film fad (*Twister, Volcano*) with a movie called *Glacier!* These narrative elements establish not only theme but also tone and voice, and many of them need to stay in the next draft, but he knows that he needs to lift scenes out of this linear history and highlight them as well as give more emphasis to the final summer.

His revision starts almost at the end of the previous draft, placing him on the road to the final tournament. "It's three a.m. Friday Labor Day weekend 1985. I left Sutton's Bay at ten p.m. headed for Houghton, which is about as far as driving to Nashville. I'm wearing my softball uniform and my wife Carole is asleep in the back seat, cotton balls stuffed in each ear while the tape deck blasts out a medley of Beach Boys and Beatles tunes—my favorite road music." But the present tense narrative of that summer experience has barely begun before Mike inserts a paragraph break, white space on the page signaling a shift of scene or time, and in the past tense recounts his initial involvement with the softball team years before. A page later he inserts another break and shifts back to the present tense and the immediate circumstances to establish that he and his wife have plane tickets for Paris which conflict with the tournament dates (a point of information barely mentioned in the earlier draft's conclusion) and that they have put off foreign travel in the past to be available for championships that never materialized. The dramatic tension in this conflict makes the reader wonder from the beginning which option they will take in the end. Telling this part of the essay in present tense heightens that tension and establishes a sense of immediacy about the experience, as if the outcome had not been decided long ago.

Throughout the remainder of the essay past tense vignettes of a softball life alternate with present tense scenes from the decisive summer. Paragraph breaks allow him to crosscut between the past and the present and to ignore connections and transitions in either chronology. When he has finished his revisions, he has avoided the linear chronology that bogged down his earlier draft and achieved a tight, dense essay with more dramatic and pointed individual segments. The overall effect of the essay is the same he had hoped to achieve in the earlier draft, but it is more focused and consequently more powerful.

The white spaces on the page—the page breaks or paragraph breaks—are part of the composition. They serve as fade-outs/fade-ins do in films, as visual cues that we have ended one sequence and gone on to another. Often, somewhere in the early part of each segment, a word or phrase serves as a marker indicating the change of time or place, very much as a superimposed title on a movie scene might inform the viewer: "Twelve years later. Northern Michigan," to suggest that a lot has happened since the screen went dark and a new image began to emerge.

In almost any contemporary collection of creative nonfiction, many selections are segmented, sectioned off by white spaces or rows of asterisks or subheadings in italics or boldface. A thematic issue of the (now-defunct) travel narrative journal *Grand Tour* has no unsegmented essays. In an issue of *Ploughshares* devoted to essays, fourteen of the twenty-three essays are segmented by paragraph breaks or, occasionally, some more pronounced method of subdividing. In a similar issue of *American Literary Review*, fifteen out of nineteen essays are segmented, their segments separated by rows of diamonds or white spaces, divided by subheadings, or numbered; only four essays are completely unsegmented.

In some of those fifteen *ALR* essays the segmenting in the fifteen is barely noticeable, almost a printer's convention rather than an actual break in the flow of thought or language; in most, however, the segmenting is emphatic, crucial. William Holtz numbers his thirteen segments in "Brother's Keeper: An Elegy" and begins eleven of them with the same sentence, "My brother now is dead," usually as the main clause in sentences with varying subordinate or coordinate elements. The repetitions give the segments the power of incantation or prayer. Lynne Sharon Schwartz, writing about translating the book *Smoke Over Birkenau*, begins her essay with a series of English words she listed in an Italian edition of the book—an opening line reads: "Strenuous. Grim. Resolute. Blithe. Alluring. Cringe. Recoil. Admonish." Occasional excerpts from the list interrupt the essay from time to time in place of asterisks or numbers or subheadings between segments ("Haggard. Cantankerous. Imploring. Dreary. Plucky. Banter. Superb. Vivacious. Snarling. Prattled."). Frederick Smock's "Anonymous: A Brief Memoir" opens with a section of Gwendolyn Brooks's poem "Jane Addams" and is divided into segments subtitled by locations in his anonymous subject's home: "The Great-Room," "The Landing," "The Dining Room," "The Grotto," and so on. Paul Gruchow's "Eight Variations on the Idea of Failure" has eight numbered sections with self-contained vignettes of varying length that thematically explore the subject of failure. These are essays that call attention to their segmentation; they announce very early on to the reader that progress through them will not be linear, although it may be sequential, and that the force of the segments will come from their juxtaposition with one another and the effect of their accumulation by the end.

These are not conventional essays, the kind that textbooks usually teach people to write, the kind that begin with some sort of thesis statement, then march through a linked, linear series of supporting, illustrative paragraphs to a predictable, forceful conclusion. Textbooks tend to teach either the unattainable and ideal or the undesirable but teachable. The segmented essay has been with us for quite some time and may well be the dominant mode of the contemporary essay, but we are only just beginning to recognize it and only haltingly beginning to teach it.

⸎

Shaken by her son's death in the crash of his Air Force jet, Carol sets out to retrace the path of his life. She and her husband drive from Michigan across the country to California, and then come back by way of the southeastern United States, all the while trying to connect to the life her son had led in scattered places. Throughout the trip she keeps a journal of her travels and eventually decides to write an essay about the journey.

As she begins writing, she finds herself hampered by the amount of detail she has accumulated about the trip, about her son's life, about her reactions to each location. So much information seems relevant and interrelated that it is difficult for her to be inclusive and yet get to the end of both the essay and the trip, where the real significance of her pilgrimage comes home to her. It is a trip of several weeks and thousands of miles and, unless she is to make it book length, which she doesn't want to do, she needs to find another way to come at this mass of strongly felt material.

Eventually she discovers the key to the composing in the materials on which she bases the essay: the narrative of the trip, the reflections in her private journal, the references to her son's life. Alternating among episodes of narration, reflection, and reference, she uses the separate strands of her materials to comment on one another and to justify her breaking off one segment to move to another. The essay begins with a passage of narration and description about the onset of the journey ("We need this trip like the desert needs rain. For months the dining area has looked like a war games planning room with maps everywhere."); it is followed by an excerpt from her journal remarking on how she feels a few days later, set in italics to identify it immediately as separate from the narrative (*"June 7. Badlands. Last night when we walked back to our campsite in true dark, stars in the sky notwithstanding, we became disoriented*"); this is followed by description of another location, further down the road ("In Wyoming, as we drive north toward Sheridan, we watch antelope standing far off. . . ."); then another excerpt from the journal; then a section reflecting her son's experiences ("Kirk loved Wyoming. In 1976 his father and I took him and his brother and sister to Yellowstone. . . ."); and so on throughout the essay. Paragraph breaks between segments and changes in font make it easy for the reader to follow the shifts and jump cuts. It becomes a travel montage with "voiceover" commentary and an alternating strand of personal history. The juxtapositions of landscape, biography, and commentary move us more quickly through the essay than full linear chronology could do, and yet the chronology is there, a beginning, a middle, and an end, given an almost cinematic force by the accumulation of a series of concentrated segments.

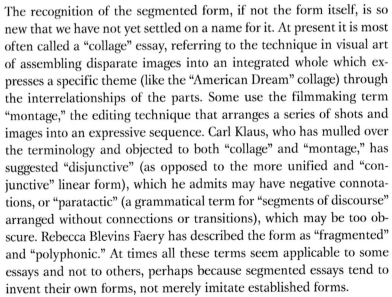

The recognition of the segmented form, if not the form itself, is so new that we have not yet settled on a name for it. At present it is most often called a "collage" essay, referring to the technique in visual art of assembling disparate images into an integrated whole which expresses a specific theme (like the "American Dream" collage) through the interrelationships of the parts. Some use the filmmaking term "montage," the editing technique that arranges a series of shots and images into an expressive sequence. Carl Klaus, who has mulled over the terminology and objected to both "collage" and "montage," has suggested "disjunctive" (as opposed to the more unified and "conjunctive" linear form), which he admits may have negative connotations, or "paratactic" (a grammatical term for "segments of discourse" arranged without connections or transitions), which may be too obscure. Rebecca Blevins Faery has described the form as "fragmented" and "polyphonic." At times all these terms seem applicable to some essays and not to others, perhaps because segmented essays tend to invent their own forms, not merely imitate established forms.

   Take, for example, "The Ideal Particle and the Great Unconformity" by Reg Saner. In this complex essay, Saner connects two terms from geology which identify two different concepts of scale. The "ideal particle" is the term for a grain of sand one tenth of a millimeter, "the size most easily airborne in wind, thus the likeliest to begin a surface effect known as saltation," where one grain strikes other grains with enough force to make them capable of becoming airborne (163); the Great Unconformity is a gigantic gap in the geological record, a place where, following the Grand Canyon walls down the deposits of millennia, you encounter a layer so much older than the layer above it that 1,200 million years of deposits must have been erased before the layers you have been following were laid down. The Great Unconformity was created by the erosive power of the ideal particle and the enormity of the span of time in the life of the planet.

But Saner is not simply explaining these two concepts as a geology textbook might readily do in a paragraph or two. Rather, he is attempting to give the reader some sense of the scale involved here as well as what it is like to experience the scale. Thus, while the essay discusses the history of geological studies and major markers for dating the planet, it also has a personal narrative running through it. Saner recounts a hike into the Grand Canyon, alternating speculations and observations about geological theory and evidence with vignettes of encounters with other hikers. In order to understand the subject of the essay as Saner understands it, the reader has to experience it with him, not simply have it explained to him.

> Slowly we accepted the curve of the earth. It dawned on us like a great change of mind, after which, earth's size came easy. Not its age. Evidence was everywhere underfoot, unmistakable. We chose not to see it.

This opening segment is a brief verbal fanfare that sounds the theme of the essay. The segments that follow alternate exposition and argument with narration and description, taking the reader deeper and deeper into both the subject matter and the experience. We dig down through the segments, like layers of sedimentary deposits, the white spaces between segments marking them like layers of geologic time. Perhaps this is a geologic essay, then, or a tectonic essay, where the segments are like plates moving and colliding and rearranging themselves on the crust of the essay.

The ability to arrange and rearrange segments frees writers to generate unique forms. Mark Rudman has created a series of essays he refers to as "mosaics," such as his "Mosaic on Walking." The mosaic metaphor suggests an essay composed of little sections, like mosaic tiles, which create a larger picture by the way they are cumulatively arranged. For example, the opening tiles are these segments separated from one another by the grouting of white space:

In this season I am often sulky, sullen, restless, withdrawn. I feel transparent, as if inhabited by the weather.

Only while walking am I relieved from distress, only then, released from the burden of self, am I free to think. I wanted to say walking brings relief from tension without sadness and then I think it is not so—these walks bring their own form of *tristesse*. There is discomfort when movement stops.

Though not exceptionally tall (a shade under six feet), I am a rangy, rambly walker. I take up a lot of space!

In "Mosaic on Walking" the sequentiality of the arrangement is difficult to perceive; it might well have been written simply by composing a random number of segments which in some way relate to the theme of walking and then either haphazardly or systematically arranging them in a disjunctive or nonsequential order on the page—the way you might copy a list of sentences about walking in the order you discovered them in *Bartlett's Familiar Quotations*. The mosaic, at least as Rudman uses it, seems lacking in design, capable of being read in any order, virtually devoid of transition or sequence; it uses an accumulation of associative segments to create mood or attitude. Maybe we should use the term "cumulative essays" or "associative essays."

But Nancy Willard, in "The Friendship Tarot," begins with the image of a tarot card arrangement on the page ("I lay out the cards of our friendship"). Each section of the essay which follows is named for a specific tarot card in that arrangement—The Child, The Journey, The Garden, The Book—and opens with a description of the picture on the card ("The card shows a child with chocolate on his face wandering through an art gallery in downtown Poughkeepsie devoted—for two weeks—to illustrations from children's books."). The segments lead us through the sequence of the tarot reading to get at issues of change and growth in a particular friendship. Perhaps it is a "tarot essay" but I don't know if the term applies to all segmented essays or, in all the history of essays, to her essay alone.

It isn't that collaging or segmenting abandons structure—it's that it builds essay structure in ways that may be organic with the subject, ways that may not be immediately recognizable but which incrementally explain themselves as the reader progresses through the essay. In the models of structure that composition textbooks traditionally provide, the ancient and venerable rhetorical topic of arrangement is handled by providing molds into which to pour the molten thought and language of the essay: comparison/contrast, thesis/support, process—all prefabricated shapes to be selected off the rack to fit the body of the topic—or the five-paragraph theme, the one-size-fits-all product of the rhetorical department store. The segmented essay, on the other hand, attempts a tailor-made design, a structure that may be appropriate only to itself.

⸺⧽⧼⸺

I am at a writer's workshop in Montana, happy to be among a talented group of writers who have brought manuscripts on the outdoors and thrilled by my first experience in the Western mountains. In the mornings we workshop one another's manuscripts under Gretel Ehrlich's directions; in the afternoon we hike the foothills of the Bitterroot Range or raft the Bitterroot River or ramble the valley floor. Late at night or early in the morning I write in my journal about the workshop sessions and the hiking, particularly where I have gone and what I have seen. In the end I have records of three hiking expeditions, one that takes me only a little way up Blodgett Canyon, one that takes me to a falls a few miles up the Mill Creek Trail, and a third that brings me to the awesome Bear Creek overlook on the shoulder of a mountain. When I try to analyze my frustrations and satisfactions about those hikes, I begin to see the possibility of an essay coming out of the experience. Back in Michigan after the workshop, tinkering sullenly with the critiqued manuscript, I drop everything and instead begin writing about my Montana hiking. I give the essay the working title "Bitterroot" but eventually call it "Knowing Where You've Been," a title inspired by a Norman Maclean story about Blodgett Canyon which had helped me set a hiking destination in the first place. Perhaps because the other essays in the workshop have so often been segmented, divided into brief episodes or scenes or vignettes, I don't consider for a moment constructing an argumentative essay built around conclusions reached and made up of rationales for reaching them. At once I understand that I have come to the conclusions I have by taking three separate hikes, each of which went successively further into the wilderness, all of which culminated at the end of the final hike with a blissful moment of triumph and contentment, with a sense of arrival I hadn't had in the earlier hikes. I wonder if I can come at this by taking my reader through the three hikes with me, taking her deeper on each hike, leading her to the same moment and the same site of discovery that I reached. In brief, I wonder if I can somehow get the reader to reach my conclusions for herself by experiencing through my prose the same things I experienced.

This is risky, I know. Gretel Ehrlich's off-hand crack about the "plodding midwestern prose" of my workshop manuscript still chafes my ego like a fresh wound I can't stop picking at long enough to let heal. If I am to make my readers hike, the hiking better be brisk, lively, and limited, and each hike better be distinctive, so that it becomes clear why they've had to do three of them. I write the hikes in present tense, to make them feel more immediate, and I start them off the same way. I chip away at narrative that fills in the gaps of time between the hikes and tighten the prose for strength and speed. I also insert reflective interludes between the hikes, past tense segments responding to the hike just completed and pointing towards the next hike.

In the end, the essay has five tight segments: hike ("The first afternoon. We walk the Blodgett Creek Trail."); interlude ("'When you look back at where you've been,' Norman Maclean writes, 'it often seems as if you have never been there or even as if there were no such place.'"); hike ("The second afternoon. We mill around after the morning workshop, plans shifting, destinations uncertain, finally resolving to go back into the mountains, to another trail."); interlude ("When I asked my friend from Montana about places to hike in the Bitterroot Valley, he looked thoughtful for a moment, shook his head, and said, 'Well, as early as you're going, there'll be too much snow to bag a peak.'"); hike ("The final afternoon. The morning workshop over, the group disperses for various tours and activities."). Each hike takes the narrator (and the reader) deeper into wilderness; each interlude raises issues that only an additional hike can resolve; the physical experiences of moving deeper and higher are echoed by intellectual and spiritual experiences, so that the physical moment of final achievement coincides with the spiritual moment of arrival. The successive drafts make me better understand exactly what it is I was feeling at the end of that hiking and push me to prepare the reader for that epiphany on the mountain ("It isn't how far at all but how deep. I need to go as deeply into wilderness as it takes before the wilderness comes into me.") in a way that makes it unnecessary for me to explain it afterward or add an epilogue of explication that breaks the reader down both physically and emotionally. The essay has to end on the mountain and the segmented format invites me to end it there.

⸺⸺

The segmented essay makes demands not only on the writer but on the reader as well. Carl Klaus has noted how segments can be read both as isolated units and as reverberating links to other segments; it is "a strange reading experience, unlike that produced by any other kind of prose" which produces in him "an irresolvable tension between two different ways of reading and responding." From reading each segment "as a discrete entity as well as . . . in connection with its immediate neighbor," he finds that his "accumulating sense of recurrent or contrastive words, phrases, images, metaphors, ideas, topics, or themes" forces him to "intuitively mak[e] connections or distinctions between and among the segments, almost as if I were experiencing some of the very same associative leaps that might have provoked the essayist to write a piece in disjunctive form." These "associative leaps" may replicate the fragmentary nature of "recollection and reflection" but they also suggest a willingness to accept unresolved or undefined associations.

Such writing demands that the reader learn to read the structure of the essay as well as its thought. That is a task for which the twentieth-century reader is well prepared, because the episodic or segmented or disjunctive sequence is a familiar design in many other genres:

- the interrelated collection of short stories—for example, a concept suggested by Hemingway with the interludes between stories in *In Our Time* or carried out in Ray Bradbury's *The Martian Chronicles*;
- the playing with chronology and the episodic structure of novels like Milan Kundera's *The Unbearable Lightness of Being* and Kurt Vonnegut's *Slaughterhouse-Five*;
- cycles of thematically linked poems, each poem separate and independent but enriched by juxtaposition with poems on similar subjects or with similar perspectives;
- the "concept" album of interlinked songs—the Beatles' *Sgt. Pepper's Lonely Hearts Club Band* or the "suite" on half of *Abbey Road*, Pink Floyd's *The Wall*, or the more loosely thematic *Nebraska* and *Born in the USA* albums of Bruce Springsteen;
- sequences of brief scenes in motion pictures—*Pulp Fiction, To Die For, The English Patient, Shine*, and *The Hours* all present their stories out of chronological sequence. In none of these is it hard to reconstruct the chronology, but telling the story in strict chronological order would have changed the emphases of these films. But even in strictly chronological films, the film progresses by sequences of shots or scenes, each separated from one another by visual cues as definite as chapter headings or theatrical intermissions.

Examples abound. It might be argued that the modern reader/viewer is more accustomed to disjunctiveness than to strict continuity.

⎯⎯ ❦ ⎯⎯

I write this essay in segments. How can I explain what the segmented essay is like, or how it comes about, in an unsegmented essay?

⎯⎯ ❦ ⎯⎯

I get up early in the morning to write, a common writer's habit. I am following a vague outline in my head of alternating segments—a more or less narrative example of someone composing a segmented essay alternating with a more or less expository section discussing the form. Practice alternates with theory. I have a lot of examples in mind that I think I might be able to use, and sometimes I type a section break or white space and insert a line of reference to spur my memory when I get to that segment ("Sandra's essay is giving her lots of trouble"; "I write this essay in segments"). Sometimes, by the time I reach that line, I have decided not to use it or have already used the example and I delete the line.

Some days I complete the draft of a segment in a single session, partly because I know I will have to revise it—go back to Mike's drafts to compare them again and to dig out more material for illustration, reread Carol's essay to refresh my memory about specific references, ask somebody about tarot readings, work on the concreteness of the language and clarity of the explanations. At first I am interested chiefly in having a structure to work in, and I have already cut and pasted segments in this draft to juxtapose them in different sequences.

Other days I only get through a portion of a segment. Some are harder than others to write, some have more detail, more development, quotes to look up and copy. I don't mind leaving them undone, because I think that when I return to them the next day my subconscious will have worked on them a little bit and it will be easier to launch into the drafting again. Even in an essay that isn't segmented we still work from section to section; it really isn't much different here.

And finally one morning when I feel I've said enough and need to worry less about finding something more to say than about finding ways to say what I've said better, I run off the full draft and try to work with what I have. Sometimes whole segments disappear or merge with others, sometimes new segments announce their necessity and have to be drafted and revised, sometimes the order of the segments changes again and again. I work harder on the language now, when I'm certain the ideas will stay. I am always reassured by a quote whose source may or may not have been Oscar Wilde: "I always revise everything eleven times, ten times to get the words right, and the eleventh time to put in that touch of spontaneity that everyone likes about my writing."

⸙

Montaigne's method for his essays—the essays that confirmed the literary possibilities of the genre—was associative: "My Style and my mind alike go rambling," he wrote. The best of our essayists working in the Montaignian tradition—for example, Phillip Lopate, Joseph Epstein, Edward Hoagland—depend on a continuous thread of free association running through their essays. They let associative links of vignette, anecdote, reference, and evidence build in hopes of discovering a thesis. Association and accumulation have always been major ways of knowing in the personal essay, and the means of drawing on these ways of knowing have expanded in our time beyond the continuous "conjunctive" flow familiar in the traditional essay to more discontinuous "disjunctive" or "segmented" forms. To understand more fully the kind of strategies that the segmented essay might use, consider two literary genres that nonfiction is seldom compared to, drama and poetry.

The segments of a work of nonfiction can be structured like scenes in works of theater or film or dramatic television. In Shakespeare's *Chronicle History of Henry the Fifth*, as in other Elizabethan and Jacobean plays, juxtaposition is the ruling method of organization, a continual leaping back and forth among at least four distinct sets of characters. The juxtaposition makes the reader or viewer compare and contrast the behaviors of the different groups, most tellingly in the scenes in the French and English encampments the night before the battle of Agincourt. In *Henry V*, again and again we are given parallel scenes rather than the simple march of exposition, complication, climax, and denouement, and by the end of the play our response has been formed more by the braiding together of juxtaposed scenes than by the working out of a single narrative arc.

Nonfiction can draw powerfully on juxtaposition as well. In her essay "Still Life" Mary Gordon juxtaposes information about the physical infirmity and mental deterioration of her aged mother against information about the life and art of Pierre Bonnard, particularly Bonnard's "The Bathroom," painted the year Gordon's mother was born. The essay is rich in juxtapositions: Bonnard's wife, dying of tuberculosis, bathed constantly; Gordon's mother, crippled in childhood by polio, never bathes; Gordon and a younger friend are devotees of saunas and swimming pools and shvitzes. Visits to her mother's nursing home and to a Bonnard exhibition make up the narrative moments of the essay, but it is the juxtaposition of the essay's segments which connects her mother's slow dying to themes of Bonnard's art and uses the artist's life and art to illuminate both the mother's progressive decline and the essayist's sense of incremental loss. The reader's engagement with the essay grows out of the juxtaposition of scenes, not from the development of a narrative that leads toward some form of closure.

The segments of an individual work of nonfiction can also be structured like stanzas in a poem or song. The work of Mary Oliver, a poet who writes verse, prose poems, and lyrical essays, exemplifies this observation. She uses white space in her prose the way she uses it in her poetry—to isolate and highlight images, actions, fragments of experience and thought. Oliver herself defines "stanza" simply as "a group of lines in a poem that is separated by an extra amount of space from other groups of lines, or other stanzas" and compares it to a "paragraph in prose, which indicates a conclusion of one thought and the beginning of another, a sensible division." She says that "a stanza break will inevitably result in either a felt hesitation or a felt acceleration." She also insists, "Any change from an established pattern indicates that the poet wants the reader to feel something different at that point. One of the assets of a pattern is this ability to 'manipulate' the reader by breaking it." She sees the stanza as "a guide to the way the poet wants the reader to feel and understand the poem" as well as "a part of the design of the poem."

Everything that Mary Oliver says about the stanza applies not only to the use of divisions in her poetry (as well as in the poetry of others) but also to her use of segments or sections in her own essays. For instance, "Sister Turtle" is divided into four numbered parts, each of which is composed of a varying number of segments (two in part I, three in part II, three in part III, two in part IV), each segment of which is composed of varying numbers of paragraphs. The opening paragraph of section I is about appetite and so is the final paragraph of section IV; the essay is a meditation on appetite and mutability with illustrative scenes from the breeding cycle of snapping turtles and the author's encounters with them. Oliver has balanced the segments of this essay as she would stanzas in a poem. If you were to take out the white spaces and read the piece as a straight run of continuous prose paragraphs, you would demolish its art and erect invisible speed bumps of discontinuity where the visible text displays seamless semantic transitions.

Scenes and stanzas can, of course, be arranged to lead the reader chronologically, in tight linear progression, as they do in any number of plays or poems, as chapters in novels often do. The associative nature of the essay, the rambles of the essayist's mind, can, of course, be expressed, as in Montaigne, by an unbroken stream-of-consciousness association of ideas, with transitions between paragraphs not always tight and clear but nonetheless continuous. This is how our minds work as well. The gaps between segments in a segmented essay are partly a visual indicator of how separate the segments are.

Part of what we do in life is assemble the associations of memory and experience and struggle to make sense of them. It's an act of discovery. This is what, on a large scale, Annie Dillard is doing in *For the Time Being*, in which she braids together strands of information on "scenes from a paleontologist's explorations in the deserts of China, the thinking of the Hasidic Jews of Eastern Europe, a natural history of sand, individual clouds and their moments in time, human birth defects, information about our generation, narrative bits from modern

Israel and China, and quizzical encounters with strangers." Whether she arrives at some ultimate conclusion—her quest in the book is essentially to discover the unknowable—the reader is forced to make associations and to consider relationships simply by being confronted with these braids of evidence.

This is pretty much the way we really encounter experience and try to make sense of it. Think of a book like one of the *Travelers' Tales* anthologies, made up of excerpts from other books, articles, essays, each with adjoining boxes of quoted material from other sources that reflect or reverberate from the main material. Think of the Internet, where we have choices of a dozen places to go on each page, individualizing and fragmenting the experience of the whole. We make sense of the world by association, accumulation, juxtaposition, just the way we make sense of the world in a photo album, a book of poetry, in a sonnet sequence, in a film like *Magnolia*, in a collection of short stories or essays, in other works formed of scenes, stanzas, and segments.

We're not locked into limited forms of writing any more than we're locked into limited forms of reading the world. We can't wait in the world for someone to come up with a clear, precise, linear explanation of events, the one right interpretation of our idiosyncratic and unpredictable lives. Why would such explanations be the only ones we can provide for other readers who read the world as we do?

NOTES FOR NONFICTIONISTS: SEGMENTING

The first thing to remember about segmenting essays is that you're simply applying an alternative set of strategies; like all other strategies or forms, it's something you do to serve your—and your readers'— understanding of your subject. Remember too that you may have to help the reader understand what segmenting is trying to achieve. Finally, remember that the terms we use, such as "collage," "montage," "mosaic," "vignette," "episode," and "segment," aren't prescriptive or formulaic, merely descriptive or comparative; we use them to suggest possibilities, just as we offer examples not as forms to slavishly fill in but as models from which a writer can intuit a useful approach. Often I advise other writers stuck in linearity and chronology, "Why don't you try collaging this?" (I like making a verb of the noun, outraging any grammarians who overhear me.) If anyone wants to better understand "collaging" or "segmenting" as composing methods, I offer the following suggestions:

- *Consider the definitions*: The terms we use to explain the "nonconjunctive" essay—"collage," "montage," "mosaic," "vignette," "episode," "segment," "disjunctive," "paratactic," "polyptych"— suggest alternative ways of approaching the form at that same time that they define distinctive variations on it.
- *Examine a variety of examples*: Many segmented essays provide readers with an immediate appreciation of the possibilities inherent in the form—for example, Nancy Willard's "The Friendship Tarot," Annie Dillard's "Living Like Weasels," Susan Allen Toth's "Going to Movies," William Holtz's "Brother's Keeper," Naomi Shihab Nye's "Three Pokes of a Thistle," Reg Saner's "The Ideal Particle and the Great Unconformity," Christine White's "Reflection Rag." Rather than establishing an explicit set of formulaic procedures, they offer writers an intuitive sense of what might happen in their own work.
- *Experiment with strategies*: Having a range of possible strategies to draw on helps writers find—or create—forms congenial with the content of their writing. Although, as we've seen, some essays are unique, one-of-a-kind works, segmented essays generally are constructed in one of several different ways—
  - by juxtaposition—arranging one item alongside another item so that they comment back and forth on one another (for example, Toth's "Going to Movies" is made up of four vignettes: three dates with different men, the fourth a solitary trip to the theater);
  - by parallelism or braiding—alternating or intertwining one continuous strand with another (a present tense strand with a past tense strand, a domestic strand with a foreign strand,

a narrative strand with a reflective strand; for example, the hiking and geology strands in Reg Saner's "The Ideal Particle and the Great Unconformity");

- by patterning—choosing an extra-literary design and arranging literary segments accordingly (for example, Willard's use of tarot cards in "The Friendship Tarot" or Frederick Smock's use of rooms in "Anonymous: A Brief Memoir");
- by accumulation—arranging a series of segments or scenes or episodes so that they add or enrich or alter meaning with each addition, perhaps reinterpreting earlier segments in later ones, up to a final segment (for example, Holtz's approach in "Brother's Keeper");
- by journaling—actually writing in episodes or reconstructing the journal experience in drafts (Gretel Ehrlich, for example, uses the journal form as a narrative device in many of her works, such as "From a Sheepherder's Notebook: Three Days" or "Cold Comfort").

Sometimes it's necessary to produce partial or full rough drafts in a linear, conjunctive, or chronological form in order to have something to convert to a segmented or disjunctive form; we have to search through the prose for elements to be arranged in a structure more appropriate to the theme or topic of the essay or article being composed. But once we're open to the possibility of the segmented essay, there's virtually no limit to the variations we can bring to the form.

Collage, montage, mosaic, vignette, episode, segment—I've never found a descriptive term for anything that, if I pressed on it, wasn't somehow incapable of bearing the weight of definitive definition. I don't worry about the most accurate term for this kind of essay, because when one writer suggests to another, "Why don't you collage this?" the writing that results may as much define the form as conform to it.

6

THIS IS WHAT
THE SPACES SAY

*Each person we meet, each place we visit, each event in
our lives, and for that matter the universe itself in its far-
flung glory, all confront us as bits of perception and
memory, inklings and intuitions, and we seem compelled
. . . to bind these scraps into a whole that makes sense.*

Scott Russell Sanders

Though the custom goes back further than we usually realize, in
our own time the most significant development in the nature of
nonfiction may well be the use of space as an element of composition. Segmented essays depend on the separation of units of prose by
spaces, usually designated by numbers or rows of asterisks or squiggly lines or simply by white breaks in text. Space has become a fundamental element of design and expression in nonfiction. Knowing
what the spaces say is vital for understanding the nonfictionist's
craft and also for appreciating the possibilities of this contemporary
genre; it also helps us to better understand the nature of truth in the
segmented essay.

⊸≫⊸

The segmented essay is like an oratorio or a concerto. The spaces are like the intervals of silence between the separate elements. Sometimes the segments of prose in an essay can be recitative, aria, duet or trio, chorus; they can be *allegro non troppo, allegro appassionato, andante, allegretto grazioso*. This is what the spaces say: In this interval of silence hold onto what you have just heard; prepare yourself to hear something different; ponder the ways these separatenesses are part of a whole. Like musical compositions, nonfiction need not be one uninterrupted melody, one movement, but can also be the arrangement of distinct and discrete miniatures, changes of tempo, sonority, melody, separated by silences. This is what the spaces say.

⊸≫⊸

The segmented essay is like a medieval altarpiece, composed of discrete panels that create a series of balances and juxtapositions rather than one continuous, unified image. Think of a triptych like Hieronymus Bosch's three-part masterpiece, *The Garden of Earthly Delights*, with its large central section displaying "The World before Noah," one side panel depicting "The Marriage of Adam and Eve," the other depicting "Hell." Think of a polyptych like Jan van Eyck's twenty-part masterpiece, *The Ghent Altarpiece*, which can be displayed opened or closed, its pairs of parallel panels widely separated, each panel framed and bordered, all set off starkly from one another. Sometimes the segments of prose in an essay can be figure studies, landscapes, allegories, separated pairs of portraits, images of context and consequence thematically linked to a central scene.

This is what the spaces say: Stand up close and ponder each image on its own; stand further back and connect each panel to another panel that completes it as a pair or contrasts with it as an opposite; encompass all of it, remaining always aware of the borders and the individual panels but inviting an impression of the whole through its parts. Like a polyptych painting, nonfiction need not be one self-contained and harmonious picture but can also be an arrangement of separate images, a *retablos* or *reredos* of scenes and portraits collectively viewed but separated by borders and frames. This is what the spaces say.

—⟞✸⟝—

The spaces in a segmented essay are like the blackouts between scenes in a motion picture, like the fade-out/fade-in, the imageless transition between disparate sequences of images, the slow dissolve that introduces a flashback, the crosscutting to parallel events. The spaces in a segmented essay are like the silences between songs on a recording, the use of emptiness in photographs to highlight or foreground images, the time lapse between two hyperlinks on a website, the time it takes to shift focus from one facet of a multi-faceted object to another, the breaks between poems in a sonnet sequence. We learn what we learn, we know what we know, we experience what we live in segments and sections, fragments, moments, movements, periods, disjunctions and juxtapositions. This is what the spaces say.

—⟞✸⟝—

The issue of truth, which seldom surfaces in other literary genres, perplexes nonfictionists. Nonfictionists begin in reality, in the hope of achieving some better understanding of the actual through writing. The inventions and manipulations of character and plot that are the hallmark of the novelist's creativity are the barriers of the nonfictionist's psychology; the willingness to settle for the fictionist's "higher truth through fabrication" negates the nonfictionist's chances of even visiting the vicinity of the kind of earthbound and actual truth that is nonfiction's special province. It's hard to know the truth—perhaps especially about our own lives; it's hard, ultimately, to explain what we experience as participants, what we observe as spectators.

In a segmented essay the truth may come in bursts, in the segments of prose that are the visible text. The segmented essay is not all continuous argument, all evidence and explanation; instead, it's a combination of pause and epiphany, silence and revelation, emptiness and edifice. This is what the spaces say: arrange the viewing of the panels so that you see their relationships in the juxtapositions rather than in a unified unbroken whole; linger your thoughts on the melody just ended before you hear the one about to begin; expect to know whatever this essay is about in the same way you know anything else, in fragments of certainty and segments of supposition, surrounded by gaps in your knowledge and borders of uncertainty. You need not fill every bit of space in order to say that you know enough; you need not write unsegmented prose in order for what you write to be truth enough. This is what the spaces say.

NOTES FOR NONFICTIONISTS: STRUCTURE

Richard Reeves once said, about a documentary script he was working on, "I can't write a screenplay. No one can. But I can write a scene, and if I write enough scenes, pretty soon I've got a screenplay." Writing is an incremental process and often the increments don't come in a strictly chronological, beginning-to-end fashion, even if in the final draft that's the way a reader will encounter them. The bigger the project, the more incremental the process.

Take for example my work-in-progress about the Rhine and the Hudson rivers. I'd read some nineteenth-century American writers who had compared the two and I was curious about what validity there had been to their comparisons when they made them and what validity there would be in those comparisons a hundred and fifty years later. The possibilities of this comparative triangulation engaged me; and I set out to explore them. So I went to the Rhine and I went to the Hudson and I gathered all kinds of background material and photographs and my travel journals and started to wrestle with the potential book.

It's been daunting. The materials I've gathered involve German and American history, geology and geography, travel literature, ecology and environmental studies, art history and theory, and personal memoir. I didn't want to write a history of two rivers, a narrative of travel on two rivers, a monograph on travel literature or landscape art, a study of riverine science. Yet somehow all these elements were present in what I'd assembled in the wings to draw upon as I compose whatever it is I'm composing. How could I conceivably leap back and forth across two continents, three centuries, six or seven disciplines and still generate a book that hangs together, that makes sense as a whole?

It was while I was stewing about this, alternately pacing pointlessly and staring stupefied at my computer screen, that I took time out to open a children's game I'd picked up in a Hudson River gift shop. It's called a "myriorama," meaning "multiple" or "ten thousand" views, and it's a collection of twenty-four scenic cards which can be arranged in any order and still produce a coherent, "perfectly harmonious" landscape. The manufacturers claim you can concoct over one and a half septillion combinations. They've dubbed it "the endless landscape." No matter what kind of scene you construct, a river runs through it, because the game is copied from one distributed in Germany in the 1830s and the scenes are reminiscent of the scenes one sees in illustrated books about the Rhine from the same period. As I shuffled the cards around and saw how my own sense of design began to emerge in the arrangements I settled on, I began to think how like all the materials I had gathered these little scenes were, how my writing on these two rivers was like trying to construct an endless landscape out of random pieces. It didn't take long to realize that I'd blundered onto a metaphor for building my book. It would be a myriorama, scenes from an endless landscape, across both time and place.

It doesn't matter whether the book that emerges out of this process ends up being the prose equivalent of a myriorama; what matters is that I have a structure that serves to set this journey in motion. Whether this is the structure that will stand at the end of the process is uncertain. I'll let the process tell me that.

The issue of structure is one every writer wrestles with on every project, even when it doesn't seem to be an issue. The first book I published was a volume in the Twayne English Authors Series, a biographical-critical study of the Restoration playwright Thomas Southerne. The format of the series provided the structure: an introductory chapter chronologically recounting the author's life and career, then chapters on individual literary works, then a conclusion discussing his accomplishment. All the Twayne volumes follow this structure, and make it easy for a novice writer to simply fill in the blanks and connect the dots. Good old chronology; good old predictable pattern. I was a new PhD, adjusting to the light of the workplace after a long time in the dark cavernous depths of grad school and I was happy to have a roadmap to follow. It helped me to write a serviceable, predictable book that fit handily into a criticism series that prided itself on uniformity.

Years later I wrote another book about another writer, E. B. White, and though I was under no contract this time and had been writing and publishing on literary and rhetorical subjects for decades, I took a similar approach to the project. I wrote an introductory chapter, something serviceable to get me started, something I knew I'd have to revise thoroughly when the rest of the book was done—I'd learned enough about writing in the intervening years to know that the introduction really needs the most work and the most revision and that it needs to be written to introduce the book (or essay or article) you've actually written rather than the one you simply hope you'll be writing. So I wrote a handy outline of the chapters to come and started on chapter 2.

Somehow chapter 2 kept expanding—it became two chapters, then three, then eight. In the end, when *E. B. White: The Emergence of an Essayist* was finished, I had an introductory chapter (as predicted, totally rewritten from scratch after the other chapters were done), eight chapters on White's development as a nonfiction writer, and a concluding chapter. There *was* a chronology to the middle eight chapters, from the start of his career to the end of his career, but, because I was interested in his composing processes as well as his work in nonfiction subgenres, the book braided together alternating chapters, first a discussion of a dominant form of work in one period of his career, then a discussion of what manuscripts and letters told us about the ways he composed that form. The act of composing the book had led me to the design for the book and, in the end, produced a structure that leads the reader through stages of White's development to a point where it is possible to make conclusions about his career. Though the reliance on chronology and critical evaluation makes this book similar in some ways to the predetermined format of *Thomas Southerne*, the design of *E. B. White: The Emergence of an Essayist* is more integral to its content, more organic to its composition. That the interval between the two books was nearly twenty years tells me I've been way too slow in learning the lessons that writing itself teaches the writer about structure. It's good to have a plan, a scheme, an outline or a roadmap; these things help you decide which section to work on. But the outline or roadmap may need to be adjusted and revised, and the writer has to stay open to that possibility. Look for the eventual structure the writing leads you to rather than let the prospective structure determine the project.

One way to investigate the problem of structure in your own manuscript is to explore how other writers have handled it under similar circumstances. I don't mean that you format your manuscript in imitation of theirs but rather that you investigate the possibilities of various approaches to your story. When I was writing *Recovering Ruth*, a book that had two storylines set a century and a half apart, people who read an early draft of a section steered me to *Beyond the Hundredth Meridian*, Wallace Stegner's book about John Wesley Powell. A good book, it pointed me in a direction I didn't want to go, which helped me learn the direction I did want to go. The writer William de-Buys advised me to read James Galvin's *The Meadow*, a wonderful book that showed me how daringly a writer could move back and forth across time. Patricia Hampl's *Spillville*, about Dvorak's stay in Spillville, Iowa, in the nineteenth century and her search for evidence of him there in the twentieth, taught me something about contrapuntal balance between segments of prose; so did Garrett Hongo's *Volcano: A Memoir of Hawai'i*. Years before, I had read Ivan Doig's *Winter Brothers: A Season at the Edge of America*, with its continuous dialogue between the journal of a nineteenth-century figure and the travels of the writer in his footsteps, and without consulting it again I felt the presence of that book in the recesses of my mind. These are quite different books, and in the end the structure of *Recovering Ruth* had to emerge from its own process, be true to its own materials, but the examples of Galvin, Hampl, Doig, and Hongo licensed a range of possibility for my work-in-progress and sanctioned finding my own structure. In the end I began to see the need to crosscut between

Ruth's story and my own, to work in parallel strands braided together in ways that echo one another, the way the juxtaposition of main plot and subplot in a Jacobean play reverberate off of one another. Following the strict chronology of her life, which was brief, I was able to ignore the chronology of my research but still end the book with a multiple conclusion—the end of her story, the end of my research, the end of our parallel paths.

In spite of the sense of structure you need to start with—the sense of having a design to build from—you should be aware that you likely will not understand the structure you end up with until near the end of the project. Then it's a matter of going back into the manuscript and jettisoning whatever works against the structure you've uncovered or substituting a new bridge or arch or column for one that will not support the weight it needs to bear. In *The Writing Life*, Annie Dillard writes, in words that have served me painfully well, "The line of words is a hammer. You hammer against the walls of your house. . . . Some of the walls are bearing walls; they have to stay, or everything will fall down. Other walls can go with impunity; you can hear the difference. Unfortunately, it is often a bearing wall that has to go. It cannot be helped. There is only one solution, which appalls you, but there it is. Knock it out. Duck." I like her construction metaphor. I've had to knock out a bearing wall in a book. It was hard to face. But the new wall was stronger, more durable at bearing the weight of the structure. Models and metaphors are often interchangeable in determining structure.

Here's one eminently practical idea for dealing with structure, one I learned by working with student writers and realized I could apply to my own. When you've finished a draft of an essay or article, number each of the paragraphs and then write the numbers down the side of a sheet of paper and after each number describe in a few words what that paragraph is about. One of the things this does is build an outline of what you've written after you've written it; the other is to make clearer the balance and sequence of the events and ideas in the draft. Is the draft out of balance—too much attention to something unimportant, not enough attention to something important? Will a reader be able to follow the structure you've created and have you given enough concrete support to the topics you've raised? Can you see the relationships among the parts? What arrangement would put the draft in better balance, fuller development, clearer narrative or argumentative line? Try the process again when you've revised the draft, as a check on what you've accomplished through revision.

This may seem like a somewhat mechanical procedure but often the writer is too close to the work-in-progress to see its limitations and needs a way of stepping back and gaining perspective. If it helps the writing, it's worth doing.

In the early days of working on *Recovering Ruth*, I showed an excerpt and an outline to a prominent editor from a major trade publishing house. She told me she liked the writing and was interested in the subject matter, but wondered what her marketing department would be able to tell bookstore people about where to catalog the book. Should this be under history? biography? regional writing? women's studies? travel? memoir? Maybe if I'd been able to make the book fit under one simple label, that editor would have been more interested. In the end, though, the design of the book emerged from an effort to meet the story's needs rather than to satisfy a marketing plan. Writers need to be willing to build the structure the writing needs them to build, even if the structure is one they never dreamed of before, like writing a myriorama.

7

IMMEDIACY

I

I am happy to be reading Peter Matthiessen's new book, *End of the Earth: Voyages to Antarctica*, a Christmas present I so much savor the anticipation of reading that I deliberately read another gift book ahead of it. So now it is mid-January when I pull the book from the nightstand, remove the bookmark, and resume Matthiessen's account of his voyages. At this point he writes:

> On this brilliant morning, as swirling snow mist shrouds Mount Paget, the pristine white snow petrel makes its first appearance of the voyage, and the beautiful Cape petrels, called *pintado* for their motley of white-spotted chocolate, and the South Georgia shag, which in various species and geographic races peers with azure eye from wave-washed rocks all around the Southern Ocean.
>
> Three humpback whales that blow and surface off the bow do not move off as the *Ioffe* comes abreast but roll easily along in no great hurry. When at last they sound, their great gleaming flukes, lined white beneath, rise in slow curves like question marks against the

white mountains all around, completing their age-old graceful arcs before sliding silently from view beneath the surface.

At noon, the vessel turns inshore past black rock reefs into Gold Harbor. Twin glaciers descend from snow horizons between peaks, in an air as clear as might be found on some frozen planet. Along the edges of the bay, at the foot of steep, bare slopes of scree and grasses, gleam the golden browns of elephants and fur seals, which are scattered the whole length of the mile-long beach and far back into the tussock on the bench behind, their yawp and rumble resonant in the vast amphitheater. In the shallows of the glacier stream where it crosses the gravel beach, 14 elephant bulls recline side by side, as snug as a fresh batch of warm loaves. Each little while, the din and cry of the marine mammals, the tidal whisper on the gravel beach, is shattered by the crack and thunder of the calving glacier, like dynamite in a rock quarry, causing frozen dust to rise where the ice has fallen.

This is only my second night reading this book and, though I ache from shoveling eight inches of lake-effect snow all around my house and though the sheets this winter night are cold even under the electric blanket, I am immediately thrilled to be back on the bow of the *Ioffe,* cruising chilly seas on my way to the Gerlache Strait off the coast of the Antarctic Peninsula, in such observant company as this. As I read on into this mid-January night, 2004, I realize from an offhand comment by Matthiessen that his voyage took place in 1998, six years before. Yet I feel that what I live vicariously on these pages is happening at the moment I read it. Yes, the description is vivid and detailed—Matthiessen is one of our greatest observers—but what most captures me is the sense of immediacy.

Thinking back over the other Matthiessen books I have read—almost all his nonfiction—I recall how cumulative his material, in several books at least, has been. In *The Birds of Heaven* he visits landscapes around the world, on several continents, locating the habitats of various species of crane; in *African Silences* he examines the devastation that has been wrought to the environment in several African countries. In these two books in particular, his research, which is very much his lived experience, has taken place over a period of many years (Matthiessen seems to be an indefatigable traveler, forever in motion), yet his prose is always as fresh, as in-the-moment, as if he were observing whatever he describes at the instant that he writes it, the instant that you read it.

The immediacy in the Antarctica book is sustained by his use of the present tense. What he describes is a past event, was in the past the morning he wrote about it on the ship (if he did), even if he was journalizing within minutes of what he saw, but the present tense captures the energy and excitement of the immediate instant. What he writes, what we read, is always happening now; on the page, at least, it will never be history, be what once happened. He could easily write, "Three humpback whales that *blew* and *surfaced* off the bow *did* not move off as the *Ioffe came* abreast but *rolled* easily along in no great hurry." Past tense tells us what took place a while ago—a few minutes or a few centuries ago—but present tense tells us what is taking place as we speak, and pulls us into the instantaneous experience.

<hr />

Perhaps I pay attention to this passage in Matthiessen because I am more aware of present tense in nonfiction lately. I think of Dagoberto Gilb's essay, "Northeast Direct," where he recounts being on a train from Boston to Penn Station in New York and noticing another passenger reading a copy of his novel. Gilb selects his own seat on the train because it has an electrical outlet where he can plug in his laptop and the essay has the flavor of being written as events occur. He recognizes the book in the other passenger's hand, muses about the improbability of the coincidence while the passenger is busy in a forward car, and describes what happens after the reader sits back down in the row ahead of him:

> He sits down. He's picked up the book! He's gone to page one and he's *reading!* Somehow I just can't believe it, and I'm typing frantically about him and this phenomenon. He's a big guy, six-two. Wire glasses, blue, unplayful eyes. Grayish hair, indicating he's most likely not an undergrad, and beneath a Brown University cap, which, because he's wearing the cap, indicates he's probably not a professor. Grad student

in English? Or he's into reading about the Southwest? Or maybe the cover has drawn him to the purchase. He's turned to page two! He's going! I have this huge smile as I'm typing. Bottom page two, and yes, his eyes shift to page three!

This blow-by-blow, page-by-page account of what he sees, apparently in the random order that events occur and that he notices details, all written in the present tense, gives me the feeling that Gilb is indeed "typing frantically" about his reader and the experience the two of them are sharing (unbeknownst to the other passenger). The essay reads like stream of consciousness, the flow of words given momentum by the flow of events, and very likely a considerable portion of this essay *was* written that way. A great deal of the sense of immediacy in the prose arises from the immediacy in the composing—this is being written as it happens.

Except—

Except that the essay ends with Gilb and his reader arriving at Penn Station and getting off the train and briefly walking side by side in the same direction through the terminal, while Gilb still ponders whether to introduce himself to the reader and concludes that he shouldn't.

> You know what? He doesn't want to talk. I am sure he has no desire to speak with me. Would definitely not want to have that conversation I'd planned. No time for me to fumble around and, maybe, eventually, tell him how I am the writer. This is New York City, no less. He's in a hurry. He'd grimace and shake his head, brush me off. He already thinks I am one of those irritating people you encounter on a trip, the one always at the edge of your sight, the one you can never seem to shake. And so as I begin a ride up the escalator toward the taxi lines, I watch him go straight ahead, both of us covered with anonymity like New England snow.

You know what? Gilb's speaking directly to me as if I were his traveling companion instead of another of his readers. Either that, or he is letting me overhear a conversation he's having with himself. That conversational "You know what?" helps with the sense of immediacy the text gives us; the past tense would demand something more formal, more decided—"As we walked briskly side by side in cold Penn Station, I realized that he didn't want to talk. He had no desire to speak with me and definitely didn't want to have that conversation I'd planned." In the past tense the ending of the essay is also less spontaneous, more contrived and self-dramatizing: "As I rode up the escalator toward the taxi lines, I watched him go straight ahead, both of us covered with anonymity like New England snow." As past tense narrative it has a staged quality, while present tense makes us feel that events as they occur are steering the narrative in the direction it goes.

But if Gilb is no longer writing on his Powerbook (which has a weak battery, which is why he needs to be anchored to an electrical outlet) and if in the narrative he is leaving Penn Station with it stowed away, when is he composing the account of the experience happening *now?* My answer is, it doesn't matter how long the gap is between the experience the essay describes and the composition of the essay (though I'm absolutely certain some portion of the rough draft of the essay *was* composed on the laptop on the train) because the electric tension and suspenseful urgency of the essay is sustained—and needs to be sustained—by the immediacy of the present tense. The story "One day I saw someone reading my book on a train and although I wanted to speak to him I didn't" probably doesn't need to be told, but the experience "I'm watching a guy on a train read my book and can't decide whether to speak to him or not" probably needs to be shared with somebody. In past tense it becomes that vaguely interesting but generally unexciting story, but in present tense it remains that surprising and exhilarating experience.

I sometimes think of this brave new world of creative nonfiction we live in as a Golden Age of the Present Tense. It seems to me that we use it a great deal more often than we used to and not always in the ways we used it in the past. For example, leafing around through my books for earlier examples of the present tense, I happen upon this one, from "A Sea Shell in Normandy," the opening essay in *The Romany Stain*, by Christopher Morley:

You first see Mont St. Michel from the toy railway train at St. Jean-le-Thomas. You know then that what you have always heard was true. After lunch at Genêts you drive across the sands at low tide, in a cart pulled by two horses. On a grey afternoon, with opal storm clouds coiling in the west, the wide floor of the bay lies wet and bare, shining all silver and fish-belly colours. The rock of Tombelaine sprawls like a drowsy mastiff on guard. You feel that if you stroked the warm granite chine he would rise, stretching, and fill the empty day with a yawn of thunder. In all that clean vacancy, framed in the blue scabbard of Normandy and Brittany, the holy boulder rises, a pinnacle of stone jewellery. The great ramps are rusted with tawny lichen. Tiny gardens niched among the steep zigzags are bright with flowers. With the genuine thrill and tingle of the pilgrim you climb, cricking your neck at the noble sheer of those walls and struts that lean upward and inward to carry the needle of the spire. Pinnacles rally and burn aloft like darts of flame. You can almost feel the whole roundness of earth poise and spin, socketed upon this stony boss of peace. You think of the Woolworth Building. How nice if that too were sown with clumps of pink and yellow blossom and had blankets of green ivy over its giraffe rump.

Morley continues in this vein throughout the essay, using the present tense and the second person to imply continuity, permanence, universal experience, though Morley was also too literary and humorous a writer not to be aware of the absurdity of implying thoughts of the Woolworth Building to everyone who visits Mont St. Michel. "You" or "we" in the present tense often intends to suggest shared, unvarying experience, but Morley doesn't appear to use the present tense to suggest the immediacy of his experience.

In Alfred Kazin's memoir, *A Walker in the City*, present tense and past tense are used in traditional ways. In the opening of the book he speaks of Brownsville, where he grew up, in the present tense:

Every time I go back to Brownsville it is as if I had never been away. From the moment I step off the train at Rockaway Avenue and smell the leak out of the men's room, then the pickles from the stand just below the subway steps, an instant rage comes over me, mixed with dread and some unexpected tenderness. It is over ten years since I left to live in "the city"—everything just out of Brownsville was always "the city." Actually I did not go very far; it was enough that I could leave Brownsville. Yet as I walk those familiarly choked streets at dusk and see the old women sitting in front of the tenements, past and present become each other's faces; I am back where I began.

The present tense here, despite the supposed confusion, is used to indicate either a continuing present (this is the way it always is because nothing changes) or the present era in which the book is being written (the present is like the past because place triggers memories that make the writer feel he is back in the past rather than in the present, where he is really a different person than the child who grew up here):

The early hopelessness burns at my face like fog the minute I get off the subway. I can smell it in the air as soon as I walk down Rockaway Avenue. It hangs over the Negro tenements in the shadows of the El-darkened street, the torn and flapping canvas sign still listing the boys who went to war, the stagnant wells of candy stores and pool parlors, the torches flaring at dusk over the vegetable stands and pushcarts, the neon-blazing fronts of liquor stores, the piles of Halvah and chocolate kisses in the windows of the candy stores next to the *News* and the *Mirror.* . . .

But when Kazin wants to talk about what actually happened to him in the past, he always uses past tense. The shift from past to present always indicates a shift from childhood to the time when the memoir is being written. This is a pretty traditional (though in Kazin's hands powerful and evocative) use of tense.

I find an interesting use of the present tense, possibly a textbook example of what grammarians call "the historical present," in E. B. White's *Here Is New York.* White was writing the essay in the summer of 1948, for *Holiday Magazine*, and by the time it became a small book the following year he was already aware of how things in the city had changed in the interval. Nonetheless White occasionally insists on the present tense to foster a sense of immediacy: "New York provides not only a continuing excitation but also a spectacle that is continuing. I wander around, re-examining this spectacle, hoping that I can put it on paper." In the pages that follow he often reverts to the present tense to describe experiences that are already past: "It is Saturday, toward the end of the afternoon. I turn through West 48th Street. From the open windows of the drum and saxophone parlors come the listless sounds of musical instruction, monstrous insect noises in the brooding field of summer. The Cort Theater is disgorging its matinee audience." Or: "It is seven o'clock and I re-examine an ex-speakeasy in East 53rd Street, with dinner in mind. A thin crowd, a summer-night buzz of fans interrupted by an occasional drink being shaken at the small bar. It is dark in here (the proprietor sees no reason for boosting his light bill just because liquor laws have changed)." In another passage he writes:

> In the café of the Lafayette, the regulars sit and talk. It is busy yet peaceful. Nursing a drink, I stare through the west windows at the Manufacturer's Trust Company and at the red brick fronts on the north side of Ninth Street, watching the red turning slowly to purple as the light dwindles. Brick buildings have a way of turning color at the end of the day, the way a red rose turns bluish as it wilts. The café is a sanctuary. The waiters are ageless and they change not. Nothing has been modernized. Notre Dame stands guard in its travel poster. The coffee is strong and full of chicory, and good.

In his foreword to the book edition of the essay White remarks on one of the changes since the previous summer: "The Lafayette Hotel, mentioned in passing, has passed despite the mention." But the description of the afternoon in the café, because it is in present tense, makes the scene immediate and ongoing rather than historic or elegiac.

<hr>

Manuals and handbooks of English usage refer to the use of the present tense to describe actions or events that clearly have taken place in the past as the "historical present." While the historical present is,

as *The American Heritage Book of English Usage* calls it, both a "legiti-
mate tense shift" and "a literary device," I think it's the wrong term
for what Matthiessen and Gilb and a host of other writers are doing
with the present tense in their writing. "Historical present tense" is a
form imbedded in past tense, used when narrative is told retrospec-
tively, after events have occurred. But these nonfiction writers—and,
as James Phelan reminds us, a good many fiction writers as well—are
presenting their narratives simultaneously, "as events are happening."
Suzanne Fleischman, offering rules for the "narrative norm," has de-
clared: "Narratives refer to specific experiences that occurred in some
past world (real or imagined) and are accordingly reported in a tense
of the PAST" (quoted in Phelan). If we think of narrative in these
terms, then what Phelan calls the simultaneous present is problematic
for us in both fiction and nonfiction, because we expect narrative
to always have the advantage of hindsight. This is especially the problem if we think of creative nonfiction exclusively in terms of fiction—
applying novelistic techniques to the recounting of factual events—or
journalism—applying reportorial techniques to the recounting of factual events—instead of in terms inclusive of all the modal possibilities
in literature. I think the simultaneous present tense in contemporary
creative nonfiction can also be termed "the lyrical present."

It is certainly a standard device in lyric poetry. Think of Frost:
"Whose woods these are I think I know. / His house is in the village
though," from "Stopping by Woods on a Snowy Evening." Think of
Yeats: "I walk through the long / schoolroom questioning," from
"Among School Children." Think of Jane Kenyon's "April Chores":
"When I take the chilly tools / from the shed's darkness, I come / out
to a world made new/by heat and light," or "The Clearing": "The dog
and I push through the ring / of dripping junipers/to enter the open
space high on the hill/where I let him off the leash." None of these
refer to current or habitual states or actions, as the present tense
supposedly does, nor are they attempts to render a specific past in a
"breathless" or "conversational" historical present. Instead, while
they *are* immediate, conveying the sense of being composed at the
moment of utterance, they are really outside of time, and that may
be what they are meant to convey.

All of these examples are written in the simple or "pure" present ("I walk") rather than the more common progressive present ("I am walking"). Susanne Langer has pointed out that the pure present "is *the tense of timelessness.*" She writes, "In literature, the pure present can create the impression of an act, yet suspend the sense of time in regard to it." Langer is chiefly referring to the use of the simple present in lyric poetry. "The whole creation in a lyric is an awareness of a subjective experience, and *the tense of subjectivity is the 'timeless' present.* . . . Lyric writing is a specialized technique that constructs an impression or an idea as something experienced, in a sort of eternal present." George T. Wright, expanding on Langer's ideas, claims that, by using it, the writer locates the action "in a realm outside our normal conscious time world, where every event must be assigned a more precise temporality." He concludes that this creates "a new aspect or tense, neither past nor present but timeless—in its feeling a lyric tense." Drawing on Wright, Susan Hunt Nelson goes a little further, declaring that "the simple present, without qualifiers or modifiers, isn't a tense at all. It's an annihilation of time. It signals a journey outside of time, beyond history, beyond consciousness." She writes, "It's the simple present tense I choose when I want to go journeying in place." Langer, Wright, and Nelson are talking specifically about lyric poetry but it seems to me that the use of the simple present in creative nonfiction arises from the same impulses—and perhaps the same practices—as in poetry. The lyrical present in nonfiction creates a sense of timeless immediacy, generates for both writer and reader the feeling that the prose is being composed on the spot.

All who write regularly often find themselves composing on the spot, with a kind of internal play-by-play announcer intoning into their consciousness like Athena into the ear of Odysseus. Whether this is mental rehearsal or immediate drafting, writers generate language in the moment of observation or experience. Back in their homes or offices or rented rooms, returned from snowy woods or dripping junipers—or an unusual trip on Amtrak or a voyage to Antarctica—they strive to recapture those immediate moments, revive them on the page with as much life as they had before their eyes. The result is conversational only in the sense that reader and writer come to occupy the same place at the same moment, like a psychologist tries to enter a patient's present tense recital of a memorable dream. The present moment extends beyond a series of actions by the narrator; it includes the world the narrator sees, the world with which the narrator interacts.

The lyrical or poetic present tense in nonfiction is a way of helping both writer and reader feel the prose is being composed on the spot. I'm pretty sure that, in drafting, it's a reliable way back into the moment. If we were to write about an event we want to remember in the past tense and then write about it again in the present tense, I suspect we would find that the present tense version is more valuable as a way to relive the experience and bring us closer to the way it was experienced to begin with. The present tense as a composing tool will generate greater immediacy and intimacy than the past tense will, simply by closing the distance between the time it took place and the time it's being written about. The question of whether to keep that moment in the present tense right through to the final draft is a separate question, but the moment has to be recovered first before the writer has to make that decision.

⎯⎯⎯⎯⎯ ⊷∞∞⊶ ⎯⎯⎯⎯⎯

I like the lyrical present tense and I use it from time to time when I think I need the sensation of immediacy or when the past tense gives a distance to events that's detrimental to the emotion or drama or psychic confusion I'm trying to convey. Occasionally an editor tells me to change present tense to past and I do and I regret it, because a certain urgency, a certain intimacy, a certain immediacy vanishes on the page, and the prose seems more remote somehow, though everything but the tense is the same. Occasionally an editor tells me to make that change and after I try it I can't see what difference it makes, which means that the lyrical present tense was contributing nothing meaningful to the prose. Sometimes too much immediacy in a piece works against it, makes the reader desperate for distance, for some perspective on events. There's no sure rule. The elements in a piece of writing need to be in sympathetic tuning with themselves, and the use of the lyrical present tense, like so many other things in writing, is another element for which you have to develop your ear.

George Wright, in an extensive analysis of the lyric tense in poetry, claims, "Lyric tense helps to elevate, to make not merely permanent but monumental and mythical that virtual experience we find at the center of the poem." In nonfiction, as in poetry, the vital question may be not "When did this happen and how can I anchor it in that moment in time?" but rather "Would this moment be better served by removing it from a specific time and giving it to the reader as something permanently timeless, permanently immediate?" If we happen to want timelessness and immediacy, then we will want to use the lyrical tense.

II

I have a scholarly bent that produces articles and monographs and a literary bent that generates creative nonfiction. I think I sometimes bring into essay and memoir the habits of article and monograph. I write not only about what I do but also about what I learn, and so I not only narrate my experiences but also contemplate their contexts. Friends sometimes chide me for the writerly voice in *this* section of an essay and the scholarly voice in *that* section. I think of the first as "the experiential voice" (it records events, experience) and the second as "the reflective voice" (it reflects on and responds to information).

Certainly some narratives never risk reflection, some reflections never include narrative; in either case they never reveal competing voices. A nonfiction writer creates a persona in one work that may differ from the persona he or she creates in another work. The problem is when, in a single work, two or more personas work against each other, shifting the tone of the work and perhaps its mode of discourse. Apparently I'm not alone in feeling—or being made to feel—that, when I juxtapose the two voices, my experiential voice and my reflective voice sometimes clash, seem to come from two different writers.

Once, discussing the switch from a narrative voice to a reflective voice, the essayist Richard Terrill made this offhand remark (or something very like it): "The way to get reflection into the writing is always to write reflectively." I couldn't tell if he was being profound or flippant—perhaps both—but his remark stayed with me and when I read an essay of his in an issue of *River Teeth*, I thought I discovered a passage that illustrates how experiential and reflective writing might work together. (The italics in this excerpt are mine.)

My car climbs a hill through a rock cut, and down the other side lies the village of Colfax, with its white water tower like a golf ball on a tee at that country club a few miles back. It appears against a green hilly background. Across the way a herd of dairy cattle takes its time to be itself. In Colfax you can find "Karaoke with Dave: 5 P.M." at the Viking Bowl. You can find at least seven churches, the names of which are listed on the sign at the edge of town: United Methodist, First Lutheran, Church of Christ, and four more names I would have to stop moving to read. The Outhouse bar lies a half block from Railroad Street. "Colfax: Half Way Between the Equator and the North Pole. 3,186 miles." *It's one of many towns to brag of this.* I wonder, *if they had to leave, which way the residents would go, pole or equator?* I like to think they'd go north. Just as Minnesota and Wisconsin carry meaning in my personal mythology, so do the concepts of north and south. *North is fewer people, in more space, and weather designed to keep them out. North is a short growing season so you can better appreciate every day of it. We shouldn't be able to control the weather. The weather is not supposed to be nice most of the time.* Do I sound WASPy in this? Do I care? *This is what North means, and thus exactly what South means is not very important because it can't mean this. Perhaps in Argentina, South means this.* But Buenos Aires is a long way from the Halfway Bar and Karaoke with Dave.

In my reading of this passage the plain text is predominantly experiential, the italicized text predominantly reflective, and some are probably both at the same time. I doubt whether it's always clear when prose is experiential or reflective, except at extremes of expression, but at least here we can see reflection rising from experience; the present tense hints that this process of intermingled observation and contemplation is happening as the author lives through the experience. The combination makes us realize that "thinking" is as much a narrative act as "doing" is.

This example blends experiential and reflective writing, and it strikes me, as I cast about for more examples, that the idea of narrating thinking is one way a writer keeps a consistent voice throughout. If you begin in narrative and then make the reflection grow out of the circumstance, you have a better chance of staying in the same persona. Peter Matthiessen, whom I cited above using the present tense, has a section where the passengers spot an orca, or "killer whale," in the Antarctic.

> Late this afternoon, emerging in slow motion from long, leaden swells perhaps a quarter mile off the starboard bow, then again abeam, then a third time off the quarter, is the great fin of a huge male "demon dolphin," accompanied by a smaller animal, female or young—the third of the three exciting species (emperor penguin, Ross seal, and orca) that we failed to observe in 1998. The black, hard, solitary monolith, scarcely wavering in its skyward thrust, *looks more like a portent than a living fin, drawing to a point the emptiness of ocean in a distillation of all life and death.* (Italics mine)

The section I've italicized in the final sentence is reflective rather than experiential: the reader is watching, with the writer, something tangible and solid, and the reflection grows out of the description. Matthiessen continues reflecting in the next paragraph, after establishing an experiential base in the first sentence: "I stare and stare. What could have been the evolutionary purpose of such an astounding apparatus, six feet high or better?" He muses on the question he asks himself and in the third paragraph of this section gives us further information about orca populations, their ranges, and their feeding habits, before concluding the section in a sentence that identifies the type of orca being viewed and simultaneously connects us back to the narrative: "The animals seen this afternoon more than 500 miles from the nearest coast are the ocean hunters."

Reflective writing tends to be present tense writing—you're talking about how things are or how they appear to you to be—but it isn't always immediate. Often in writing, even in personal essay or memoir, let alone in cultural criticism and literary reportage, it is necessary to provide information or to theorize about events or attitudes. Academic writing and informational writing very often pride themselves on the exclusion of the "I": refusing to acknowledge the individual author who is generating the prose and using a declarative persona that intones facts and ideas like some remote, disembodied voice overlooking the universe. In other words, sounding something like the last two sentences—note that I seem to suggest that these things take place without human intervention, even though in all writing it is always the first person who is speaking. While it may not be necessary to the topic to include a first person persona, I think it's always dangerous to write by any blanket rule that excludes the possibility of doing something, because the writer's job is to figure out what's best for the writing, not to make the writing merely as good as it can be within arbitrary and timid rules of conformity and regularity.

Consider two more examples of immediacy in reflective writing. Donald M. Murray, in *My Twice-Lived Life*, is essentially writing a book of reflections about aging. He includes many narrative moments, including an account of the heart attack that made him consider retirement and reevaluate his priorities, but most of the book consists of musings about aspects of life that senior citizens have to deal with. In one passage in a chapter about work—Murray is a Pulitzer Prize–winning journalist, an innovative writing teacher, and a successful columnist—he writes:

> Work is our play. I can still remember playing with blocks or with my lead soldiers on the living room rug or coloring in a book or organizing my stamps or building a tower with my Lincoln Logs or Erector set or reading, passing from this life into the world of story, and jumping when someone spoke. I have been lost to the world in the concentration of play. And as we get old, as our imaginary fears become reality, as we make appointments with yet another specialist, wait for the results of yet another test, I still know the blessing of concentration, of work. Minnie Mae comes down to my writing desk, speaks, and I jump, leaving my chair, shaking as I fall back down to my seat. I have not been where I appeared, an old man at work, but had escaped into the country of work, where all my attention is focused on the task, the

solving of a familiar problem that has become wonderfully unfamiliar in its doing.

Murray, it seems to me, is letting narrative arise from reflection. The instances and anecdotes that appear in this passage are concrete illustrations of abstract ideas; they reinforce the ideas by placing them in specific contexts, making it possible for the reader to understand how they operate in an actual world rather than in a theoretical one. It surely would be possible to express the ideas without the incidents—"Work and play exhibit similar dimensions of concentration which, at certain levels of actualization, may involve the transference of consciousness of space from a physical location to a psychological site and occasion a disorientation or sense of dislocation when concentration is interrupted by occurrences in actuality."—but not without a loss of immediacy. Reading my revision one might well ask, "Like when?" Murray has made the answer to that clear and made the experience real and immediate.

Murray is writing in the first person singular and the instance of his jumping at his wife's approach is another example of the historical present. Simon Winchester, the author of popular works of history like *The Professor and the Madman, The Map That Changed the World, Krakatoa,* and *The Meaning of Everything,* usually writes in the third person and is not very much given to writing in the present tense except when the information is current and continuing. *The Meaning of Everything: The Story of the Oxford English Dictionary* is a book recording a series of events in intellectual history that led to the completion of a massive undertaking. The book is often about individual editors and contributors but it is also about the English language and a dictionary. Winchester's job, since he is writing nonfiction for the general reader and not solely for linguists and lexicographers, is to make a work of exposition and reflection sustain a narrative flow. Here is the opening paragraph:

> The English language—so vast, so sprawling, so wonderfully unwieldy, so subtle, and now in its never-ending fullness so undeniably magnificent—is in its essence the language of invasion. It was always bound to be so:

geology and oceanography saw to it that the British Isles, since long before their populated time, were indeed almost always islands, and the ancestors of all who ever lived there first arrived by sea from beyond, bringing with them their customs, their looks—and their languages.

The paragraph is a good one to read aloud, so that the reader notices the places where dashes, commas, periods, and colons, the full arsenal of punctuation, are put to work regulating the flow of the sentences. Winchester is covering a great deal of ground here, the sweep of British history, the scope of the English language, but his syntax creates a sense of immediacy to the prose. The dashes in particular but the active voice throughout and the use of the colon to set off a simple declarative main clause ("It was always bound to be so:") and the everyday English of the vocabulary all create a conversational directness and liveliness to the passage that Winchester generally sustains throughout the book. In spite of being a book largely in the past tense about an impersonal subject, Winchester is able to generate a sense of immediacy that invites the reader into the experience.

<hr />

I ask myself, now that I'm near the end of a long chapter on the subject, just whether I should emphasize—and make my readers consider—the element of immediacy this much. I ask myself as well, scrolling back over pages replete with examples from other writers, whether I avoided, when I made those selections, writings lacking in immediacy. Sometimes when we're working up a subject, particularly one that grew out of unexamined earlier observations, we find reinforcement for our ideas everywhere we turn; it's as if we are suddenly hyperconscious of a trait to which we'd earlier been oblivious. Certainly the use of present tense worked on me that way. In recent nights, reading a translation of Victor Hugo's *The Rhine*, I've been startled by moments when the author abruptly abandons the past tense in which he has been narrating his travels to present the scene in the historical present, as if deliberately providing me an ideal example to put in an article. The question is whether, in our hyperconscious state, we're assessing the circumstances in the accurate proportions.

I wonder now: on those occasions when people felt I wrote in two voices, one writerly, one non-writerly, were the voices not simply experiential and reflective but rather immediate and non-immediate (or whatever the opposite of immediate is)? If immediacy can be created in the past tense as well as in the present, is there a range of immediacy that the writer can tune in? On this end the hyper-immediate, on that end the minimally immediate, the lyrical present occupying a large chunk of this end, the vivid past occupying much of that end? Is there a point where immediacy vanishes into warp-immediacy at this end and evaporates into non-immediacy at that end? Probably. Are non-immediate forms of prose valid and permissible? Sure.

I come around by my wrestling with these questions—at the moment, immediately—to feeling that the issue may not be one of immediacy but one of the tension between dynamic and static states of prose. Generally I'm put off by hyperactive prose, the kind that creates a sort of essay-on-speed and presents dynamic prose as a kind of extreme sport; I'm also put off by moribund prose, the kind that creates a sort of essay-in-granite and presents ponderous prose as a kind of verbal tectonics. If writers on either end of this spectrum want to connect with a limited, exclusive readership expert at reading either hyperactive or moribund prose, that's fine with me, but I'd rather read—and write—prose that goes to neither of these extremes. The space in between these extremes is very wide and offers countless locations on which to situate the writing. On any of those locations we might find an alert, attentive, lively writer creating vivid, vibrant, dynamic prose that helps the reader not simply connect with the subject, whatever it is, but inhabit it in the way the writer does.

Perhaps, in the end, that's what I mean by immediacy.

NOTES FOR NONFICTIONISTS: IMMEDIACY

Here's a situation for you centered on present tense and past tense. I went off on a quick tour of an area of Colorado to follow the trail of an earlier writer. Because I was driving and was intending to cover the route in one day—Isabella Bird rode for weeks on horseback in 1873—I frequently spoke my observations aloud into a tape recorder and as I drove. It was immediate; I was where I was when I was talking about where I was. I wasn't trying to compose as I traveled, merely trying to record as much information and as many on-the-spot reactions as I could. At home I transcribed the audiotape onto my computer verbatim, exactly as I'd spoken it. I also spent portions of the next several days writing a very long journal entry as a chronological narrative of the trip from beginning to end. Because the tour was over and I was recalling it as I wrote in the journal, it was in past tense. When I finished the journal entry in longhand, I transcribed it word for word into the computer in a separate file from the tape transcript. I also typed in a number of extended quotes from the writings of Isabella Bird and some of her contemporaries who had traveled in the same locations. All of this was simply prewriting, preliminary compilation of materials to draw from in the subsequent composing. By merging and revising these various files I hoped to draft a couple of chapters about my trip.

Question: Should I write in present tense or past tense? My trip is over, it's in the past, but my tape transcript of my travels is permanently in the present. There can be no confusion either way—both a reader and the writer know the trip is over—so the issue is whether immediacy would add to or detract from or do neither to the telling.

There may be some advantages to taking readers along with me as the trip is happening. For one thing, it makes clearer the distinction between the earlier writer's trip (past tense) and mine (present tense). For another, it helps me avoid making the chapters too long and too information-packed and gives readers a better sense of what my trip was like for me or would have been like for them had they been with me. The disadvantage might be that describing things as they're happening makes it easy for the prose to get "marchy," as Sarah Dickerson, a friend who read this material, terms it. She means it tends to go sequentially step-by-step to preserve forward momentum for its own sake, faithful to the order of events as everything happened, rather than skip the lulls and focus on the highlights.

She's generally been right about passages she's labeled in the margins as "marchy."

The only way to resolve this is to try writing sections of it either way. Since the chapters are divided into sections about specific locales I can change everything from present to past or past to present and see which one sounds best, is most involving without doing any damage to the facts. I can also determine, with each approach, whether the narrative flow is sufficiently smooth and strong, where impediments need to be removed or the pace slowed, whether the prose simultaneously does the most justice to the material and the best service to the reader.

The situation I've been describing suggests ways any nonfictionist can experiment with immediacy. One way is to look over a draft of something you've already written in past tense and find a scene to convert to present tense. You can simply get rid of all the past tense markers—like the "ed" endings on verbs—and add present tense markers where necessary—like the "s" endings on verbs—but this will likely be at least somewhat unsatisfying; the prose will need more changes than that to seem organic. Or you can read through the passage and then rewrite the scene again in the present tense, from scratch, without consulting the original again. That gives you two (more or less) organic versions to compare. Which version do you think works best?

You can also reverse the process. In effect, since journals (or logs or daybooks) are often written in present tense and narratives in past tense, this kind of conversion is what writers who write on-the-spot entries and fieldnotes routinely do. Find a present tense scene you've already written and rewrite it in past tense. What's gained or lost by the change?

Or consider a scene you haven't written yet but intend to write. Write the scene both ways and make the comparison. (Going back to an earlier chapter, find a photograph and write about it in past tense and then write about it in present tense. What do the various approaches do to your understanding of the moment the photo records?)

Comparing versions of your own text in present tense and past tense to see which way works best, not only for the writing but also for the reading, you'll likely find that the preferable version—and there may not always be one—will be the one that works best in the context of the project as a whole. Immediacy is a literary strategy that is sometimes irrelevant or counterproductive, but frequently it is vital to a composition. Being aware of how other writers use it and being alert to its possibilities in your own compositions makes it more likely that you'll be able to use it effectively.

8

DISTANCE

I

The composition scholar Sue Lorch once wrote about a transforming experience in her writing life, composing a college paper about a painting. She described her confidence going to the Fine Arts Building "to knock out with grace, alacrity, and ease [her] first paper" for a college English class. She located the painting she and her classmates were assigned to describe and, in her words, "sailed up, sat down, and let the words flow. What could be so difficult about describing an oil on canvas depicting a few cows standing in a field surrounded by trees, I wondered. . . . I left some thirty minutes later, my one-draft, sure-fire A paper stowed in my knapsack." When, a few days later, her paper was returned with an F, her first instinct was to "look up whatever rules of good writing I had inadvertently violated, observe them" and essentially correct the paper as her effort at revision. But the teacher hadn't found those kinds of errors in her paper; instead he had failed her for being boring. She tried a variety of approaches to enliven her paper but at first felt no need to go view the painting again. After all, she says, "I had the most complete, albeit boring, description of it that anyone could wish. I had described it in meticulous detail, top to bottom, left to right, down to counting the spots on the cows." She muses further:

> Not for life, love, or sacred honor (a concept intimately tied in my mind with the need to make As) could I conceive of the means whereby I could make my description more interesting. The painting wasn't interesting; it was, after all, of a bunch of cows standing in a nondescript field, and images of pastoral perfection and bucolic bliss did not accord with my view of the world in 1968. As the pile of yellow paper at my feet grew deeper, my mood grew darker. I was going to have to take myself to see that so-called art again, through the rain this time, and I didn't want to. I was bored into a near coma by the thing the first time I saw it, and the second time could only be . . . Whoa. Wait. What had I just said? Could it be that my paper was boring because I had been bored? Had something of me inadvertently crept into a paper about a picture? Now I was in deep trouble. Not only did I have to go look at it, I was going to have to become interested in it.

In the end she discovers that the painting is subtly ironic, that instead of "promot[ing] an image of the world as pastorally perfect or bucolically blissful," the painting "suggested the tenuousness, the fragility of such tranquility and peace."

Sue Lorch remembers this experience as one that taught her a great deal about the complexity of "communicating effectively to another human being," the intricacies of composing process and rhetorical situation. *I* think—this is *my* interpretation of *her* experience—that it also demonstrates the vital necessity of engagement, of personal commitment, as an element of writing. It wasn't enough for her to simply look at the picture; she had to see it, which takes a different level of involvement. Her example confirms my experience over decades of teaching: student failure at writing is less often a result of inability or dysfunction than a result of indifference or disinterest or disengagement, the half-hearted effort of a first-and-final draft hacked out during back-to-back episodes of "Friends" or "The Real World," the time-serving somnambulism of those who intend to get a degree but don't expect their education to, like, overlap into their real lives.

In writing, the eye of the beholder has to be open, has to endeavor to behold. It's not enough to look; you have to see. A writer has to become immersed in the subject, not intent on keeping her distance from it.

II

"We commonly do not remember that it is, after all, always the first person that is speaking," Thoreau tells us, and claims, "I, on my side, require of every writer, first or last, a simple and sincere account of his own life, and not merely what he has heard of other men's lives; some such account as he would send to his kindred from a distant land; for if he has lived sincerely, it must have been in a distant land to me." Thoreau also observed, "Only that day dawns to which we are awake." His phrases haunt me when I think about writing.

I do not take Thoreau to mean that the first person singular pronoun needs to be overtly present in every text but that every writer's presence has to be. It's no trick to eliminate the pronouns but the writer him- or herself cannot be absent. Only that writing is meaningful to which the writer is awake, as Sue Lorch's testimony tells us.

Even what Robert Coles calls "documentary work" isn't the simple task of recording reality undiluted; "with the best tape recorder in the world, with cameras that take superb pictures, and even with a clear idea of what I am to do," Coles says,

> still I face the matter of looking *and* overlooking, paying instant heed *and* letting something slip by; and I face the matter of sorting out what I *have* noticed, of arranging it for emphasis—the matter, really, of *composition*, be it verbal or visual, the matter of re-presenting; . . . Stories heard or seen now have to turn into stories put together with some guiding intelligence and discrimination: I must select *what* ought to be present; decide on the *tone* of the presentation, its *atmosphere* or *mood*. These words can be as elusive as they are compelling. . . .

An individual engages and examines, responds to and reflects upon—in essence, beholds—subject matter, whether personal or non-personal, academic or non-academic. Engagement brings the writer closer to the subject, evaporates the detachment of distance.

Efforts to eliminate the individual writer produce a noncommittal kind of nondiscourse, the kind of writing Ken Macrorie so long ago labeled "engfish," the kind of evasive, dishonest writing examined by George Orwell in "Politics and the English Language" and by Richard Ohmann and Wallace Douglas in *English in America*. The essayist Scott Russell Sanders has decried the "murky" and "anonymous prose that mumbles like elevator music in the background of our industrial civilization—the prose of memos, quarterly reports, grant proposals, program summaries, newscasts, run-of-the-mill journalism, court briefs, perfunctory scholarship, and tidy English papers." These expressions of horror over depersonalized, dehumanized, deliberately obfuscational writing are, unfortunately, still relevant, as is *Philosophy & Literature*'s annual Bad Writing Award for prose which seems to seek the highest levels of density, abstraction, and polysyllabification and the greatest length of chains of prepositional phrases in nominalized terms of least common currency in narrowest dissemination—the kind of academic writing whose point, according to editor Dennis Dutton, is to "beat readers into submission. . . . Actual communication has nothing to do with it."

That's the point about nondiscourse—it doesn't try to have a dialogue with the reader but attempts to exclude the largest possible number of readers from the discussion. Some people can, of course, read this stuff—or at least apparently can, since a lot of it gets published—but I, for one, can't and I've given up trying. I haven't been beaten into submission, but I've certainly felt bludgeoned by this language and convinced that the writer doesn't want to talk to me. That's all right—there are many fields in which I can't read the articles and monographs; I'm just sorry that so much of my own academic field tends to be among them. Not only can I not read much of that writing, I can't teach anyone how to write it. The curious thing for me has been listening to students trying to write nondiscourse who can't really explain what they've written and who defend themselves by saying, "But that's the way we write in my field."

I think this is a crucial point. As an editor or a teacher my job is not directive, guiding each writer to conformity with some universal style, assuring a homogeneity of textual product; rather my job is to recommend approaches to specific works-in-progress that help individual writers achieve personal objectives. The question for me isn't "How can I make this writer's text more similar to every other text I see?" but "How can this writer ratchet up the writing to a level where it accomplishes what it needs to, where it matches the writer's aspirations for it?" But, in order to have aspirations or personal objectives, writers need to be engaged in the writing; they have to become not merely bystanders but beholders.

III

In *Honey from Stone: A Naturalist's Search for God*, Chet Raymo writes,

Surely the self is more than substance, more than form. The "I" must surely be the *conscious* thing, the reluctant philosopher, the makeshift theologian. Let me shake that conscious "self" out like a basket of laundry; what do I find? Here is the cardboard game of "Chutes and Ladders" that I played at the age of four (my earliest memory). And here are the cupboards on my grandmother's porch that are filled with dark medicinal jars of pickles and jams (and here is that other terrifying jar in the shelf in the high school biology lab). Here, tumbling from the basket, are the verses of poems I memorized at the age of ten. And the guilts and raptures of adolescence. Here are novels I read in college. And the residue theorem of the theory of complex variables (miraculous! beautiful!). The trajectory of Comet Swift-Tuttle. Devonian deltas and Carboniferous seas. The spectrum of Vega. And more. Much more. Where did it all come from? How did it all fit into so small a basket? . . .

It hardly makes sense to think on it. The self swims in intricacy. Whatever the "I" is, it is as small as a hazelnut and as large as the universe.

Raymo is a professor of physics and astronomy whose book is a geological-astronomical-spiritual-personal travel memoir, a work of stunning insight and dazzling prose. *Honey from Stone* and another of his books, *The Soul of Night*, reaffirm what, for me at least, academic life has too often seemed to deny: it's alright to have a self; in fact, it's not only alright, it's unavoidable.

It isn't a question of whether or not first person singular pronouns occur in the writer's text. As Scott Russell Sanders observes, "Even when the self is not on display, an actual, flesh-and-blood human being still composes the sentences, and writers well trained in the first-person singular are likelier to feel a responsibility for the accuracy and impact of their words."

It's not only the "eye" of the beholder that makes the difference; it's the "I" of the beholder as well. Chet Raymo ends the segment from which the passage above is taken with this sentence:

> I will sit on this starlit bank and shiver in my ignorance, red blood pouring through my veins, a wind of atoms blowing in and out through my nostrils and the pores of my skin, pummeled with particles from the cores of stars, Vega-drenched, sandstone-lifted, terrified, unconsoled, undefined, ecstatic.

That's a sentence to read aloud. I read it and I think, I wish I could write like an astronomer—this astronomer and physicist, at least.

IV

So. Writers can't be bystanders, can't be detached and remote from whatever they're writing about, be it their own lives, art in a museum, or the nature of the universe. They have to be beholders, and beholders generally have two courses open to them. They can be either participants or spectators.

A participant is a writer who has lived the life in the writing, participated in the travel, the experiences, the events, the lives of the other characters. In familiar essays, memoirs, narratives of travel and nature, we expect to be participating along with the narrator or author. A spectator (as opposed to a bystander, who may be present but neither involved nor attentive) is an engaged observer. In reportage, literary journalism, ethnography, and cultural reflection we expect to be observing along with the writer, having access to what the writer knows and learns and making judgments about the information with an awareness of what informs the writer's judgments.

These are not mutually exclusive roles. A memoirist must often be a spectator as well as a participant, step back away from the immediate and try to be an objective observer at times. A reporter must often be a participant as well as a spectator, plunge into the environment he's reporting on sometimes and be conscious of its effects on him. In neither case can writers kid themselves that they are not present, that they are not implicated, in what they write and what they write about.

It's really a question of distance. It's like being in a theater. If you sit too far from the stage or screen, you can't figure out what's going on; you miss nuances and gestures and expressions and keys to interpretation. If you sit too close, you can't take it all in; you are overwhelmed by disproportionate attention to miniscule detail, lose all grasp of the big picture. Instead you need to find an appropriate middle ground, somewhere that suits your vision and level of engagement, where you can take in both scale and scope, content and context. Where you sit depends on the kind of beholder you are and the kind of production you're beholding.

V

Some nonfiction theorists worry a great deal about writers keeping their distance from the subject, because they see nonfiction as a factual field and factuality as something that can be assured by distance, detachment, objectivity. They want to preserve the validity of academic scholarship or the reliability of journalistic reporting (I'm not using either term ironically) while still employing the artistry, the aesthetic qualities, of literature. Clearly I'm more skeptical about the validity of scholarship and the reliability of reporting than they are, particularly when writers are too detached and too distant, but I'm not interested in giving much attention here to the problems of writing in specialized disciplines or in arguing at length for academic and journalistic writers to adhere more to the standards of nonfictionists. It's obvious that I think my sweeping and flexible view of nonfiction has application to all writing, from first-year-composition assignments to journalism and scholarship—that is, I think that the elements of nonfiction are essentially the same as the elements of those writing provinces with which nonfiction's borders overlap. Even if I acknowledge that writers have to be aware of the discourse communities for which they're writing—and I do—I think we're all better off when discourse is as inclusive as possible rather than exclusive, and I think the writing is better when neither the writer nor the reader is kept at too great a distance.

If I haven't made it clear before, I'll clarify it now: although nonfiction is not necessarily about the self, the self is implicated in all nonfiction, including nonfiction that is ostensibly scholarship or reportage. Let me offer some examples.

The book I cited earlier, *Honey from Stone*, by Chet Raymo, is an excellent example of a book that is both thoroughly learned and thoroughly literary. I found it on the "Physics" shelf in the back of my local bookstore, with a retailer's tag that labeled it "Science History" and a publisher's line on the back cover that labeled it "Science/Nature & Outdoors/Travel/Spirituality." The book is set on a location the author has been visiting for decades, the Dingle Peninsula of Ireland, which juts out into the Atlantic Ocean. A good deal of the book is about the geological origins of the peninsula and the travels of landmasses through plate tectonics. But the book is also about astronomy and the creation of the planet itself and the relation of the planet and the creatures on it to the rest of the universe. It is also about religion, including the history of religion in Ireland, and the relationship of religion and science. It is also about the author's observations of earth and sky while wandering the Dingle Peninsula. Obviously, the book is difficult to classify with one simple label, but actually that's true of a great many nonfiction books. Obviously, too, the reader can learn a great deal from the book.

What makes the book literary nonfiction then is not its subject matter, though the subject matter doesn't exclude it from being literary nonfiction, but rather the way in which these varied elements are braided together. The book is organized around hours of the liturgical day, from Matins and Lauds through Vespers and Compline, and the progress of the day is paralleled by the progress of the creation of the universe and the formation of landforms on earth and also by the creation stories of the Old Testament and culminates in the exploration of the self quoted earlier. It's a profound and complex book as well as a brilliant literary work, all of this accomplished through the merging of "objective" science and "subjective" interpretation. Even if Raymo as a character never showed up on the page, the ability and inclination to bring these varied subjects together is an individual accomplishment, growing not only out of intellect but also out of passion.

Some scholars in composition and rhetoric have suggested various names for this kind of nonfiction—for example, I tend to use the term "personal cultural criticism," Peter Elbow refers to it as "personal expressive academic writing," and Marianna Torgovnick has written about "experimental critical writing." What we're all searching for is a way to validate writing about subject matter that doesn't attempt to disguise the consciousness of its author. In her introduction to an anthology of cultural criticism that she edited, *Eloquent Obsessions: Writing Cultural Criticism*, Torgovnick hopes that the volume "will encourage writerly models for writing about culture." Heading her six convictions underlying the collection are these two (her italics): "*Writing about culture is personal*. Writers find their material in experience as well as books, and they leave a personal imprint on their subjects." "*Writing about culture is informed*. . . . Just because writing comes from the heart does not mean it comes off the top of the head." Torgovnick's convictions include a belief that cultural criticism should be, at least part of the time, less exclusive—that is, less directed at a limited audience, less dismissive of personal experience and perspective. Her approach, and that of the writers in her anthology, opens doors for writers and readers alike and expands the scope of the cultural critical dialogue.

In essence, this kind of perspective acknowledges creative nonfiction as a reflective form of writing, and links it back to the familiar essay of the past, which often was not about narrative experience but about the author's reading and reflection. This too was part of Montaigne's legacy to the essay as a literary form, and it can be traced through Addison and Steele, Lamb and Hazlitt, right up to practitioners like Joseph Epstein and Cynthia Ozick. Further examples come immediately to mind.

The personal cultural criticism in Rebecca Solnit's *River of Shadows: Eadweard Muybridge and the Technological Wild West* is unique in its approach to its subject. A host of other scholars in photography and media studies and sociology have written on Eadweard Muybridge, the nineteenth-century photographer who is best known for his motion studies on humans and animals (he proved that a galloping horse has all four feet off the ground at the same time). Solnit's approach is not only multi-disciplinary, cutting across history, media, art, and psychology, but also literary, creating the kind of personal cultural criticism Marianna Torgovnick refers to in her collection. When Solnit researches the site of one of Muybridge's photographs, the Lava Beds where the Modoc warrior Captain Jack fought American troops, she discovers that it is close to the site of the Tule Lake Internment Camp, where Japanese Americans were held during World War II and where she finds people still living. She also learns that George Takei, the actor who played Lieutenant Sulu on the original "Star Trek" series, was born in the camp. A string of associations have arisen unbidden for her, the odd juxtaposition of the last stand of the Modocs with the internment of non-European Americans less than a hundred years later and the connection with all of that to a futuristic television series adapting formulaic elements of western motion pictures which arose out of an art form that was considerably influenced by Eadweard Muybridge's experiments with photographing motion—his zoopraxiscope was able to project a rapid series of still photographs in such a way to make it appear that the viewer was watching individuals in motion, a fundamental principle of cinema. By bringing together a host of cultural references Solnit connects Muybridge to a world of art and history that we may all agree need to be connected but that hadn't been connected until this remarkable writer—this individual with her distinctive background and particular curiosities—demonstrated the links among them. Reflective nonfiction of the kind I'm illustrating (and I'm well aware of the limitations of such a term) can be located as well in such works as W. G. Sebald's *The Rings of Saturn*, Jane Tompkins's *West of Everything*, and Marianna Torgovnick's *Crossing Ocean Parkway*. Sebald's book is, oddly enough, always identified as a novel, but as Vivian Gornick has demonstrated, it's really a very quirky memoir, in which the narrator starts off talking about episodes in a long walking tour of the east coast of England and digresses into biographical and historical discussions of the places and personalities he encounters along the way. The topics that arise include the Jacobean essayist Thomas Browne, the explorer Roger Casement and the writer Joseph Conrad, the bombing of German and English cities during World War II, the natural history of the herring, and many others. It is an associative tour through the writer's mind. Jane Tompkins, writing of the Western in fiction and film, includes a remarkable chapter, "At the Buffalo Bill Museum," which examines the various elements of a Western history complex, the historical contexts in which the exhibits can be viewed, and the author's own perplexed reaction to them. It is a scholarly piece of cultural criticism without ever denying that an individual intellect is behind the perceiving. Marianna Torgovnick's book is especially interesting because in the first half she offers memoiristic essays about growing up in the Italian-American enclave in Bensonhurst—a kind of personal ethnography—and in the second half analyzes artifacts of American culture through the particular lens of "an Italian-American daughter," which generates unique insights into such topics as Mario Puzo's *The Godfather* and the personality of the Italian-American critic Camille Paglia. There is nothing unscholarly about these works except the eschewing of secondary sources, exclusive disciplinary dialects, and aloof or absent personas. They are thoughtful, researched, reflective, but also openly personal and committed. Personal here doesn't mean solipsistic or egocentric; it merely acknowledges the essential involvement of the individual writer in discovery and expression. If we positioned these writers on some sort of continuum between the poles of memoir and monograph, we would find them in various locations, some closer to one pole, some closer to the other. But none of them reach either extreme.

We could establish some similar kind of continuum for reportorial nonfiction as well, with autobiography at one end, a kind of reporting on the self, and daily journalism on the other, a kind of reporting on events drawn from interviews with others and investigation of documentary evidence. Somewhere between those poles is a wide swath generally called literary journalism, which suggests that it too has poles—one end more journalistic than literary, one end more literary than journalistic. At some point a work is too journalistic to be literary journalism or too literary to be journalistic literature and becomes one or the other. I don't know the key to pinpointing those boundaries and don't especially want to, but I suspect the difference can be measured in terms of distance of the author from the subject.

At the time I write this the local newspapers are reporting the devastating effects of the December 2004 tsunami which killed tens of thousands of people in southeast Asia. All of the articles have been cobbled together from other sources, foreign correspondents, foreign news services, eyewitness testimony, personal videotapes. The articles tend to have certain slants, depending on which section of the newspaper they're in—the business section seems to be happy that the region is so poverty stricken since that has kept down the losses in investments, insurance, and property; the sports section is mostly concerned about the experiences of prominent soccer players and skiers; the front page highlights the death of a local woman vacationing in Thailand. This is, in the main, reliable, predictable daily journalism. In a year or two publishers will release survivor stories and storm overviews; at least one will likely be titled *Tsunami!* and be touted as "in the tradition of *The Perfect Storm.*" Though all will *report* the tsunami in one way or another, some will remain book-length journalism and others—and not only memoirs—will be full-fledged creative nonfiction. The difference will depend not on the subject matter, which will be roughly the same for all, but rather on the way the writer interacts with the subject and the distance from which it is engaged.

Les Standiford's book on Henry Flagler's railroad to Key West, *Last Train to Paradise*, draws its strength as nonfiction from the author's thorough and conscientious imagining of events. Standiford, a novelist who has also written about Florida cities, brings a fictionist's sense of narrative to the history of the building of the Key West railroad. Flagler, one of the most influential figures in Florida history, began the project in 1905. It was a massive undertaking crossing stretches of ocean between the separate islands of the Florida Keys. The work was intermittently interrupted by hurricanes and eventually overturned by the great hurricane of 1935. Standiford has gripping material to work with, and the book can be compared in some ways to books in several separate subgenres. Like Ross King's *Brunelleschi's Dome: How A Renaissance Genius Reinvented Architecture*, Simon Winchester's *The Map That Changed the World: William Smith and the Birth of Modern Geology*, and Dava Sobel's *Longitude: The True Story of a Lone Genius Who Solved the Greatest Scientific Problem of His Time*, *Last Train to Paradise*, which also has a long subtitle, *Henry Flagler and the Spectacular Rise and Fall of the Railroad That Crossed an Ocean*, recounts a trajectory of groundbreaking accomplishment in which a man's visionary ambition reaches fruition. Since it also dramatizes the 1935 hurricane that destroyed the railroad, it is also a storm story, in which human beings are pitted against overpowering forces of nature, the focus of popular books like Sebastian Junger's *The Perfect Storm*, Erik Larson's *Isaac's Storm*, and, in a slightly different vein, Jon Krakauer's *Into Thin Air*, about climbers facing devastating weather conditions on Mount Everest. (I should emphasize that every one of these books, no matter in which subgenre I've placed it, is unique in its own way, demonstrating a range of possibility within similar subject matter rather than a predictable formula endlessly replicated.) The Key West Railroad story has also been written up by academic writers as history and as biography, by writers establishing greater distance between themselves and the subject and, consequently, between their readers and the subject. By beginning with the approach of the 1935 hurricane and then flashing back to tell the story of the railroad from the beginning, Standiford adopts a technique familiar from such films as *Citizen Kane*, where the main character dies in the opening sequence, and builds a tandem suspense about the outcome of both the storm and the construction of the railroad. History already knows the outcome; Standiford helps the reader live through the events while suspending their certainty about the outcome. We are moved closer to the experience of the book.

I could cite other writers, such as John McPhee or Peter Matthiessen, whose books are richly informative and yet artfully written, but perhaps the examples above will serve. Readers who encounter these examples will see that, while both reflective and reportorial nonfiction are principally informative, in the way that scholarly or journalistic works are, they are also notably literary, by virtue of their language, structure, design, and attention to aesthetics. Such nonfiction may be more accessible to a general reader than academic nonfiction is likely to be, even when both focus on the same subject, and it is more literary and reflective than journalistic nonfiction is. I don't want to press distinctions very hard, however, because not only are they difficult to isolate but they are also unnecessary for writers or readers, all of whom can decide for themselves how much distance they want to have between themselves and the nonfiction they write or read.

NOTES FOR NONFICTIONISTS: DISTANCE

One way to observe the effect of distance is to be alert to it in what you read. A technical writer friend of mine once told me how she and several other writers were assigned to write repair manuals for the military. Her approach is always to take on an assignment like that as an opportunity to thoroughly learn something she knows nothing about and then explain it for people like herself who come to the topic equally in the dark. One of the other writers tried a simpler, easier method: he cribbed liberally from other manuals and put together one that he himself couldn't have followed. He thought that it wasn't important if *he* understood it, that it only mattered if others who had to use it could follow it, and, for whatever reason, must have assumed that he didn't need to understand it in order to write a manual others would understand. However, the military brought the writers and their manuals to a base where teams of novice mechanics were given the manuals and expected to make repairs or adjustments to various vehicles as the manuals instructed. My friend's manual acquitted itself without a hitch; she hadn't simply written a manual—she'd taught herself how to do the job she was describing. The other writer came under considerable criticism when mechanics discovered that many of his instructions didn't apply to the vehicles they were working on or the problems they needed to solve.

My friend was writing an instruction manual. Clearly there's little room for the first person singular in such writing. But nonetheless she couldn't allow the distance she was expected to maintain on the page to influence the distance she maintained from her subject. Her immersion, her deep involvement in the subject, and her colleague's remoteness, his shallow engagement, were evident in the results. To the indifferent reader both manuals likely read as manuals usually do; to the informed reader one clearly was useful and the other wasn't. The varying results had to do with the distance each writer insisted on keeping from the subject, not with the distance of the author's persona from the page.

Any writer can have difficulty explaining a topic with which he's unfamiliar; it's important not to attempt to camouflage your lack of understanding by boldly trying to sound like you know what you're talking about. It's essential that the writer be honest with himself about what he knows and what he's trying to convey. When in doubt have others read what you've written to see if they understand it; in the case of highly specialized passages, ask readers with expert knowledge to judge the accuracy as well as the clarity.

Another way of looking at this issue is to ask yourself when you're reading what the author's relationship with his subject is. A good way to do this is to read a couple of works that are similar in subject and think about each author's distance from the subject on the page. For example, Simon Winchester has written two books on the making of the Oxford English Dictionary, but his presentation is different in each. *The Professor and the Madman* is a braided narrative about the intertwined lives of two very different men; *The Meaning of Everything* is far more focused on the intricacies of the dictionary's creation and has a more academic tone. For another example, Peter Matthiessen's *The Snow Leopard*, about wandering in the Himalayas in hopes of sighting a rare and elusive animal, and George B. Schaller's *Stones of Silence*, about an animal biologist's travels in the Himalayas, are quite different books, even though the two authors were part of the same expedition—Matthiessen is more literary, narrative, and reflective, Schaller is more scientific, expository, and referential. In none of these cases are we considering which is the better book or for that matter which book reveals the author's distance from the subject; these are cases where the difference lies in the distance the author takes from center stage, the degree to which he foregrounds his presence or places it somewhere in the background, even to the point of invisibility.

My inclination in writing is not to rely on learning my lessons well and trusting myself to always thereafter follow the most prudent, sensible, or expeditious course of action; instead, my inclination is to confront things head on and repeatedly make myself aware of my processes. That's why I keep a couple of different journals, so that, in addition to composing new writing, I also often make myself consider what I'm doing in my writing. Thinking about the communication triangle is one way to make myself do that.

The communication triangle is a diagrammatic way of looking at the relationship between three elements of discourse: a speaker or writer, a listener or reader, and a subject. Each of these is an angle on the triangle; each connects to the other two elements. To put the triangle into practice consider each of the angles in terms of what you're writing: What's your relationship to the subject? If you chose the subject, why? If you didn't, how can you connect to it? What's your relationship to the reader? Are you hoping to inform the reader? confide in the reader? What do you want the reader to get out of reading about this subject? Who do you want the reader to think you are? Who do you want to represent yourself as being? Finally, what kind of communication do you want all this to add up to? Something moving? reflective? persuasive? informative?

These are essentially questions of rhetoric. Rhetoric is fundamental to any communication. Think of the differences in the way you present yourself and the way you converse when you communicate with your parents, your friends, your significant other, your work superior, your contacts in daily life when you shop or commute or interact in the community. We all make automatic adjustments according to who we are, what we're talking about, who we're talking to, why we're talking, how we want our conversation to be received. It's no different in our writing—we are seldom the exact same person on the page in all the things we write.

If, taking this approach or another, we confront our connection to the writing, we are less likely to unknowingly be distant from our subject and more certain that we've adjusted appropriately to the demands of the communication we're working on. If we can determine how distant we appear to be on the page or how distant we are from what we're writing, we can take steps to close the gaps by deeper immersion—seeing rather than looking at the subject, seeing rather than overlooking our relationship to the page.

9

WRITING BY EAR

. . . the truth is I write by ear, always with difficulty and seldom with any exact notion of what is taking place under the hood.

E. B. White, "Will Strunk"

Style is an increment in writing. When we speak of Fitzgerald's style, we don't mean his command of the relative pronoun, we mean the sound his words make on paper. Every writer, by the way he uses the language, reveals something of his spirit, his habits, his capacities, his bias. This is inevitable, as well as enjoyable. All writing is communication; creative writing is communication through revelation—it is the Self escaping into the open. No writer long remains incognito.

William Strunk Jr. and E. B. White,
The Elements of Style

When I was an undergraduate, earnestly pecking out poetry and plays and short stories and a humor column and drama reviews on a portable manual typewriter, I took a writing course from William Melvin Kelley, the novelist, who had come to teach on our campus for a semester. Kelley had been the student of Archibald MacLeish, the poet, who taught that poetry is formed in the ear. Kelley, in turn, insisted that prose was also formed in the ear. It was one of my earliest craft lessons and one that I repeatedly find evidence for in the writing I admire most.

Take, for example, the writing of E. B. White, whose drafts and revisions I've examined in great detail. White had studied at Cornell University with William Strunk Jr., who had written a writing guide, *The Elements of Style*, which Strunk always referred as "the little book." It was self-published in 1918, then published by Houghton Mifflin in 1919, and revised a few more times over the course of Strunk's career. In 1957, White was sent a copy of the "little book" by a former classmate at Cornell and as he read it made notes for himself on what he was reacting to. At one point he jotted down in longhand the following (I've cut the crossed-out words and false starts in the manuscript and cleaned up the punctuation a bit):

> If I were ever faced with the (to me) impossible assignment of facing a class of students, I think I would just say, "Now you boys & girls get your hooks in a copy of the 'little book' & you go home & come back in 2 weeks. Memorize the rules, & see if you can understand some of the explanations. Come back in 2 weeks, & we will go on from there."

It is simply a spontaneous reaction to re-reading the book and reacting to the images of his professor that it conjured up. The repetition of "come back in 2 weeks" is a good sign that he's writing a zero or discovery draft, something to help him figure out what he's thinking, something that lets him experiment with language a little. Even in my slightly edited version of it, it can't be mistaken for a polished, finished passage.

Perhaps White was already thinking he might write something about the book—at that time he was often contributing pieces to *The*

New Yorker under the general title "Letters from the East" and always on the lookout for new ideas—but at some point he wrote to his classmate for more information and started drafting a piece about Strunk. The language of the longhand note reappeared in the drafts, including the passage above. In one typed draft he wrote this (again I've tidied up some):

> I think, though, that if I were ever in the, to me, unthinkable position of facing a class in English usage and style, I would lean far over the desk o[n] the first day, clutch my lapels, blink my eyes, and intone: "Get the <u>little</u> book, Get the <u>little</u> book, Get the <u>little</u> book." Then I would dismiss the class for two weeks, and tell them to come back when they had learned the rules of the game.

The draft gives lots of evidence of White revising as he composed; because he knew it was only a draft and only when he was finished would he have to turn in a more or less neatly typed copy of the final draft to the printer, he wasn't worried about typos, misspellings, or changes of mind about the language. He's still working with the idea of himself in the unlikely role of teacher, and the description of his posture and the repetition of the phrase "the little book" are meant to portray him imitating Strunk's typical posture and habit of repetition from nearly four decades earlier. Additional drafts changed the passage again and eventually the essay was published, first in *The New Yorker* in 1957 and then in the collection *The Points of My Compass* in 1962. The final version of the passage reads:

> I think, though, that if I suddenly found myself in the, to me, unthinkable position of facing a class in English usage and style, I would simply lean far out over the desk, clutch my lapels, blink my eyes, and say, "Get the *little* book! Get the *little* book! Get the *little* book!"

True, the original idea for the passage came to him early on in the process of engaging himself with his subject, but the stages the language of the passage went through suggest a great deal about White's tendency to, as he claimed, write by ear.

Reading the three indented versions of the passage aloud, we can hear the conversational shifts of emphasis in each version. In the first two versions notice how the ideas that follow the repetition of "the little book" simply limp away, trail off, drag on. The final version is much more direct, more emphatic, more memorable. The ideas underlying the passage haven't changed significantly—some of what he explicitly tells students in the first two versions is rather made implicit in the final version—but the changes affect the rhythm, the flow, the force of the sentence. In this example we can see what White meant when he confessed, after taking on the role of grammarian or rhetorician to revise Strunk's book, "I write by ear, always with difficulty and seldom with any exact notion of what is taking place under the hood."

I find examples of writing by ear all through White's work. Let me share a couple more that have made an impact on me.

White wrote a monthly department for *Harper's Magazine* from 1938 until 1943, and World War II, even before the United States entered it, was an undercurrent in the series even when it wasn't the topic of a particular piece. White later collected a selected and somewhat revised series of columns in *One Man's Meat* (the great essay "Once More to the Lake" was written for this series) and one of the passages that I find most striking in the book comes from a piece he titled "Songbirds." This is another passage to read aloud, paying particular attention to the final sentence.

> It has been an early spring and an eerie one. Already we have had evenings which have seemed more like July than April, as though summer were born prematurely and needed special care. Tonight is such a night. The warmth of afternoon held over through suppertime, and now the air has grown still. In the barnyard, among the wisps of dry straw which make a pattern on the brown earth, the sheep lie motionless and as yet unshorn, their great ruffs giving them a regal appearance, their placidity seemingly induced by the steady crying of the frogs. And in the east beyond the lilac and beyond the barn and beyond the bay and behind the deepening hills, in slow and splendid surprise, rises the bomber's moon.

White introduces an air of anticipation into a tranquil country scene—he lived on a farm on the coast of Maine—and concludes the description on an ominous note. The final sentence seems Shakespearean to me, in the sense that, like Shakespeare, White is controlling the word order and the rhythm of the phrases, using repetition and alliteration and assonance to guide the pace and reverberations of the words, in order to create a very specific final effect. The subject of the sentence is "moon" and it is the last word in the sentence. By beginning with "And" and marching through a series of prepositional phrases that create an image almost like a slow zoom or pan across a landscape—"beyond the lilac and beyond the barn and beyond the bay and behind the deepening hills," three three-word phrases linked by "and" and concluded with a four-word phrase lengthened by the word "deepening"—and then pausing to insert in commas the parenthetical and stately "in slow and splendid surprise," White builds suspense over the verb and the subject. "Bomber's moon" has an ominous percussive sound—he's suggesting that the full moon makes the tranquil landscape an ideal target for attacking aircraft—and the disturbing note of foreboding, of anxiety, is strengthened by the plosive sounds of the words. White is not simply recording a moment here; he is orchestrating the music of its language.

White has a similar passage in an essay from the same collection titled "Morningtime and Eveningtime"—the title alludes to the dreamy mood of the Gershwin song "Summertime" from *Porgy and Bess*—and is notable also as a description of a writer having difficulty writing because of a preoccupation with outside events and a jumpy distractibility. The phrase at the end—"And after lunch the thunder in the north."—is reminiscent of the "bomber's moon" sentence in "Songbirds." Reading this passage aloud, notice the long sequence of sentences that begins "You write something . . ." and the punctuation throughout, especially the two sentence fragments that close the passage:

> Stonily I sit at the machine, refusing, as a jumping horse refuses the hurdle. All that comes forth I drop without regret into the wastebasket; nothing seems to make sense, no matter how you spell it or arrange the words. You write something that sounds informative, throwing the words around in the usual manner, then you put your head out the door, or somebody puts his head in, a knob is turned,

somebody says something to you, or your eye is caught by something in the news, a dog barks, and no longer is what you said informative, or even sensible. At the mere barking of a dog the thing explodes in your hands, and you look down at your hands. As though you had crushed a light bulb and your hands were bleeding slightly. And after lunch the thunder in the north.

White has been deliberate in putting a period after "you look down at your hands" and starting the next phrase as if it were a new sentence. But grammatically speaking it isn't a new sentence; it's a phrase modifying "look down at your hands" by explaining the kind of look you might be giving your hands. An over-zealous or grammatically uptight editor might attempt to change the punctuation, make it read "you look down at your hands, as though you had crushed . . . ," but clearly that is not the effect White wants here. He wants the reader to feel a little frisson of disorientation through the unexpected syntax, a feeling that helps the reader inhabit the experience in the passage.

I could go on at length about White's ability to tune his language so that the words and phrases vibrate sympathetically (and in fact, I have, in a book on White as an essayist), but anyone reading these passages aloud already has a good idea of what it means to be writing by ear.

> *A well-known writer got collared by a university student who asked, "Do you think I could be a writer?"*
> *"Well," the writer said, "I don't know. Do you like sentences?"*
>
> Annie Dillard, *The Writing Life*

It's a dangerous thing to suggest to people generally that usage and style are matters of correctness. When White revised Strunk, reviewers were divided about the book— journalists tended to like the prescriptiveness of the Strunk sections, compositionists tended to like the flexibility of the chapter White added, "An Approach to

Style," and what one group didn't like were the very sections that the other group thought most valuable. The book itself has sold very well over the years—a fourth edition, with uncredited editorial revisions, was published in 1999, fourteen years after White's death, fifty-three years after Strunk's—because most of the advice is generally practical and much of it is useful. But too often *The Elements of Style* and, even more assertively, a host of competing books seem to be attempting to enforce a universal concept of style that, if it actually were successful, would make all writers indistinguishable from one another in terms of language. If we think about the things White does in the examples we've already looked at, we realize that he doesn't write like someone following a rulebook but rather like someone writing by ear.

One of the things I most admire about White's children's book *Charlotte's Web* is the way he uses all the techniques of his adult writing as he writes for young readers. My favorite example is this passage describing summer, which, though the book is fiction, could as easily be a nonfiction passage. It should be read aloud:

> Early summer days are a jubilee time for birds. In the fields, around the house, in the barn, in the woods, in the swamp—everywhere love and songs and nests and eggs. From the edge of the woods, the white-throated sparrow (which must come all the way from Boston) calls, "Oh, Peabody, Peabody, Peabody!" On an apple bough, the phoebe teeters and wags its tail and says, "Phoebe, phoe-bee!" The song sparrow, who knows how brief and lovely life is, says, "Sweet, sweet, sweet interlude; sweet, sweet, sweet interlude." If you enter the barn, the swallows swoop down from their nests and scold. "Cheeky, cheeky!" they say.

These are not simple sentences in watered-down language. The second sentence is incomplete, a series of prepositional phrases separated by a dash from a sentence fragment and items in a series each joined by "and" rather than a comma. The third sentence includes an observation (actually a joke) in parentheses—most readers pronounce "Peabody" as "pee-BOD-ee" but if you're from New England, or if you're a white-throated sparrow, you pronounce it "PEE-buh-dee."

The fourth sentence makes the song sparrow's call not only ono-matopoeic but also philosophical. The fifth is a complex sentence. The sentences are not uniform in length or structure and there's something more than fact to the information we get from the passage. This tendency to make the language do something more than re-port information is an important element in creative nonfiction. Take one of my favorite passages from Annie Dillard's *Pilgrim at Tinker Creek*, for example. The narrator is talking about an experience in the fifth grade where a teacher put a cocoon in a mason jar and waited for it to transform into a moth, but didn't realize that the Polyphemus moth that would emerge would be too large for the jar. Because it couldn't open its wings to dry them, the wings stayed folded on its back until they hardened into an angular hump and were impossible to open. One day, on the playground, at recess, the narrator watches the moth being released. In the most direct, most simple form, she *could* write: "As I returned to the classroom I watched the moth walk away down the driveway." Instead, this is what she *does* write:

> He heaved himself down the asphalt driveway by infinite degrees, un-wavering. His hideous crumpled wings lay glued and rucked on his back, perfectly still now, like a collapsed tent. The bell rang twice; I had to go. The moth was receding down the driveway, dragging on. I went; I ran inside. The Polyphemus moth is still crawling down the driveway, crawling down the driveway hunched, crawling down the driveway on six furred feet, forever.

When the passage is read aloud it's easy to notice that the sentences about the narrator are short and simple and spare and the sentences about the moth are long and cumulative and evocative. The moth, which can only creep rather than fly and is not meant for long-distance walking, takes longer to get to the end of a sentence than the narrator, who is swift, brisk, fleet. The sentence that is most striking is the final one, where she repeats the phrase "crawling down the driveway" three times; the traditional version might read, "The Polyphemus moth is still crawling down the driveway hunched, on six furred feet, forever," but the repetitions make the sentence repeat itself, as on a tape loop, with new details accumulating on each loop (which is part of the point of her telling this story in the first place). The language doesn't just explain the experience; it replicates it, and the sentences make the moth's departure agonizingly slow.

Dillard has a different but nonetheless memorable moth story to tell in *Holy the Firm*. The narrator, who has been camping in the Blue Ridge Mountains and reading a biography of the poet Rimbaud, observes the death of a moth in a candle by which she is reading. Reading this passage aloud, listen to the way the sounds of the words imitate the sounds of the actions being described:

> One night a moth flew into the candle, was caught, burnt dry, and held. I must have been staring at the candle, or maybe I looked up when a shadow crossed my page; at any rate, I saw it all. A golden female moth, a biggish one with a two-inch wingspan, flapped into the fire, dropped her abdomen into the wet wax, stuck, flamed, frazzled and fried in a second. Her moving wings ignited like tissue paper, enlarging the circle of light in the clearing and creating out of the darkness the sudden blue sleeves of my sweater, the green leaves of jewelweed by my side, the ragged red trunk of a pine. At once the light contracted again and the moth's wings vanished in a fine, foul smoke. At the same time her six legs clawed, curled, blackened and ceased, disappearing utterly. And her head jerked in spasms, making a spattering noise; her antennae crisped and burned away and her heaving mouth parts crackled like pistol fire. When it was all over, her head was, so far as I could determine, gone, gone the long way of her wings and legs.

The details are vivid and slow down the action she's witnessing; the actual event might not have taken as long as it takes us to read the passage. This is a good example of bringing the reader into the experience so powerfully that the reader seems to live through it as much as the writer does.

If we simply wanted an example of vivid description, this passage would serve nicely, but we should also be aware that Dillard isn't simply making us live through the experience for its own sake. Her book is about spirituality and this section is about connecting with the spirit of dedication that is necessary, according to Dillard, in both the religious person and the artistic person. In the scene she presents to us the moth ends up serving as a candlewick, and she is able to continue reading by the moth candle's light. She writes of the moth:

> She burned for two hours without changing, without bending or leaning—only glowing within, like a building fire glimpsed through silhouetted walls, like a hollow saint, like a flame-faced virgin gone to God, while I read by her light, kindled, while Rimbaud in Paris burnt out his brains in a thousand poems, while night pooled wetly at my feet.

Another terrific sentence and one that connects through allusion and metaphor the physical event of the moth's entanglement in the candle, the religious dedication of saints and martyrs, and the writer's absorption in creativity, as exemplified by Dillard's reading and her own writing. As marvelous as these examples are as language, their flare and dexterity is serving the larger issues of the work in which it appears; it isn't simply showing off for its own sake.

―――∞∞∞―――

Writing every book, the writer must solve two problems: Can it be done? and, Can I do it? Every book has an intrinsic impossibility, which its writer discovers as soon as his first excitement dwindles. The problem is structural; it is insoluble; it is why no one can ever write this book. Complex stories, essays, and poems have this problem, too—the prohibitive structural defect the writer wishes he had never noticed. He writes in spite of that. He finds ways to minimize the difficulty; he strengthens other virtues; he cantilevers the whole narrative out into thin air, and it holds. And if it can be done, then he can do it, and only he. For there is nothing in the material for this book that suggests to anyone but him alone its possibilities for meaning and feeling.

Annie Dillard, *The Writing Life*

Here's something about language and structure in creative nonfiction. Jo Ann Beard opens her essay "Cousins" with a scene in which she and her cousin are both embryos in the womb of two sisters fishing on a small boat. At one point in the narrative the narrator's aunt catches a fish. This is the scene:

It is five A.M. A duck stands up, shakes out its feathers, and peers above the still grass at the edge of the water. The skin of the lake twitches suddenly and a fish springs loose into the air, drops back down with a flat splash. Ripples move across the surface like radio waves. The sun hoists itself up and gets busy, laying a sparkling rug across the water, burning the beads of dew off the reeds, baking the tops of our mothers' heads. One puts on sunglasses and the other a plaid fishing cap with a wide brim.

In the cold dark underwater, a long fish with a tattered tail discovers something interesting. He circles once and then has his breakfast before becoming theirs. As he breaks from the water to the air he twists hard, sending out a cold spray, sparks of green light. My aunt reels him in, triumphant, and grins at her sister, big teeth in a friendly mouth.

"Why, you dirty rotten so-and-so," my mother says admiringly.

One of the things we can say to people who worry about the issue of truth in creative nonfiction, since Beard's writing is strongly narrative and fiction-like, is that, no, Jo Ann Beard isn't reporting what she knows from direct observation here—she was, after all, an embryo—but everything she presents here is retrievable information: she may have seen dated photos of that particular outing, which would give one set of details; she may have heard reminiscences of the day by her mother or aunt; she may have observed similar days herself and have direct knowledge of the behaviors of ducks and fish and sunshine on water and reeds. There is a felt truth about the scene, an imaginative re-creation of an actual moment that the writer invests with metaphysical weight.

But the reason I bring the scene up at all is to say something about the way Beard's crafting of the scene here is important for later scenes in the essay. The narrator describes a community parade of children that she, her cousin Wendell, and their sisters are in. The younger girls walk alongside their bicycles with carefully dressed dolls in the baskets; the older girls are dressed like baton twirlers and have been warned not to throw their batons into the air. Beard writes:

> The street is brilliant in the sun, and the children move in slow motion, dresses, cowboy hats, tap shoes, the long yellow teeth of the mean ponies. At the count of four, one of our sisters loses control, throws her baton high in the air and stops, one hand out to catch it when it comes back down.
>
> For a long, gleaming moment it hangs there, a silver hyphen against the hot sky. Over the hectic heads of the children and the smooth blue-and-white blur of crepe-papered spokes and handlebar streamers, above the squinting smiles and upturned eyes, a silver baton rises miraculously, lingers for a moment against the sun, and then drops back down, into the waiting hand.

These two paragraphs repeat the pattern of the two from the opening of the essay, the first preparing us for the second, the separation giving emphasis and force to the image at the center of each second paragraph, the fish and the baton, both in midair. In the second paragraph about the baton, the first sentence establishes the idea that the baton "hangs there." The second sentence, by holding off the main clause with two long prepositional phrases ("*Over* the hectic heads of the children and the smooth blue-and-white blur of crepe-papered spokes and handlebar streamers, *above* the squinting smiles and upturned eyes"), keeps the baton suspended, as does the main clause with its compound predicate ("*rises* miraculously, *lingers* for a moment against the sun, and then *drops* back down") and the comma after "down," which gives an additional pause before the baton falls "into the waiting hand." This is one of those instances where a sentence doesn't simply tell what happened ("One of our sisters threw a baton high into the air and caught it when it came back down") but in effect replicates the experience, makes us live through the experience.

For me that sentence alone is worth the price of admission to the essay, but Beard isn't simply showing off her virtuosity in that passage. It harkens back to the first scene of the essay, with its airborne fish, and foreshadows the final scene of the essay, a parallel moment when the sisters of the opening scene are alone in the hospital room of the narrator's mother. (Both segments begin with the words: "Here is a scene.") The two talk, the aunt knitting while the mother grows groggy from an injection and starts imagining things: "She's drifting now, floating upward, her shot is taking effect. She gets a glimpse of something and then loses it, like a fish swimming in and out of view in the darkness under water. She struggles to the surface." The water images link amniotic fluid and lake and hallucination:

> Her father bends over the bed to kiss her, as substantial as air; he's a ghost, they won't leave her alone. She moves slowly through the fluid and brings a thought to the surface. "We carried ours low and look what we got." They swim through her lake, gray-eyed sisters, thin-legged and mouthy. They fight and hold hands, trade shoes and dresses, marry beautiful tall men, and have daughters together, two dark-eyed cousins, thin-legged and mouthy. A fish splashes, a silver arc against the blue sky, its scales like sequins. She startles awake.

The fish imagery and silver imagery continue throughout the segment and the essay ends with this depiction of the mother's dreams.

> My mother sleeps silently while my aunt thinks. As the invisible hands tend to her, she dives and comes up, breaks free of the water. A few feet over a fish leaps again, high in the air. Her arms move lazily back and forth, holding her up, and as she watches, the fish is transformed. High above the water, it rises like a silver baton, presses itself against the blue August sky, and refuses to drop back down.

The essay, which is a long one, has been exploring the relationships between the two sisters over the course of their two daughters' lives. This paragraph links central images of both the sisters' relationship and the cousins' relationship and this motif running through the essay creates a network out of disparate and widely varied scenes. The narrator doesn't need to explain what's happening, only to narrate events and invoke in the reader emotional responses to certain moments. The fish and the baton may be artifacts of their lives but the narrator has given them symbolic weight, has made sense of them as emblems of certain elements of life. The images have energy, vitality, ebullience; they suggest irrepressibility, aspiration, liberation, transformation.

This essay of commonplace experiences is elevated by the writer's ability to discover the reverberations generated by the images of her life. Getting it into the language of the essay reproduces those reverberations in her readers.

—————

Here's something else about language and structure in nonfiction. Michele Morano opens her essay "The Queimada" with this paragraph:

> And later, after the mussels, after the pulpo a la gallega, the swirling bits of octopus flesh in a sauce of garlic and tomatoes, after the glasses of wine and loaves of bread broken and passed hand to hand, after the strong local blue cheese spread thick on thin crackers and the apples drizzled with honey, after we have all eaten as much as we can and then picked the remains from one another's plates, tucking into our mouths one more bite, one more spoonful, one more tangy or sweet or salty fingertip, then we turn, lights dimmed and candles aflame, to the Queimada.

This is a very long sentence, a string of prepositional phrases leading finally to the main clause ("we turn to the Queimada") which itself is interrupted by the insertion about the lighting. It is very deliberate, this sentence, and creates a mouthwatering sense of anticipation for what follows. I am also struck by her beginning with "And later," as if she has already been telling this story and we are already her intimates.

"The Queimada" has four sections, divided by simple paragraph breaks, and after each white space the new segment begins with the words "And later" and a reference to the Queimada she and her friends are drinking, before she veers away into other memories of these people and this experience. It is a tactic for keeping disparate elements of her experience in Spain with this circle of friends connected and also a way of immediately bringing the reader into the intimacy of this group and these memories.

—⊶⊷—

When I was young and trying to learn to play the guitar, I was constantly thwarted by an inability to hear when the strings were in tune—that is, I had a good idea when they weren't in tune but no amount of turning the tuning pegs and plucking the strings would get me near the point where the strings were in tune with one other or with a pitch pipe or piano key. I just couldn't hear it. But eventually, through watching a television series on the folk guitar and learning how to use a tuning fork, I began to understand tuning; better yet, I came to understand sympathetic tuning, the idea that I could see as well as hear when strings are tune with one another—if I could tune one string to a tuning fork or a piano, I could tune all the other strings by making each vibrate sympathetically with another.

No clear, simple rules exist to make it easy for a writer to achieve the kind of effects achieved by the authors of the prose that I've been suggesting should be read aloud. It takes an ear for language, but that can be developed, just like the ability to use sympathetic tuning on a guitar. As the writer in Annie Dillard's anecdote asks, "Do you like sentences?" writers need to like sentences and sequences of sentences and feel that their language has something to do with their meaning. I'd hope that, if asked for their own favorite passages in the writing they read, most writers could find passages equivalent to the ones I've been reproducing, sentences and paragraphs that not only resonate in the mind but also reverberate in the ear. What separates literary or creative nonfiction from anti-literary or non-creative nonfiction—all the forms of "prose-that-is-not-fiction" that I haven't been talking about—is a concern for prose style that goes beyond the conventional, the grammatically correct, the regimented. But it's not simply an issue of art; fundamentally, it's an issue of communication.

I hope any readers who don't already have a passage in mind will start listening to the writing they read, as well as listening to their own writing.

CHAPTER 9

NOTES FOR NONFICTIONISTS: WRITING BY EAR

Reading passages aloud is a valuable thing to do with literature. With drama, of course, speaking Shakespeare's language or any dramatist's text helps a reader understand something about the texture and tone of the dialogue, but it also helps with fiction and poetry. Read aloud the opening pages of "A Rose for Emily" by William Faulkner and "Hills Like White Elephants" by Ernest Hemingway, for example, and you recognize at once fundamental differences between the writers. You can hear things about the rhythm, pace, rhetoric of the language, even if you can't quite put your finger on what accounts for the difference. I think that a writer like Marcel Proust demands to be read aloud, since the sentences are so complex and rich and dense that they seem at first glance to be impenetrable and impossible to sustain but always turn out to be intricately balanced and delicately paced. My wife and I have read all the Harry Potter books aloud, and I'm not sure that we'd enjoy them so much if we weren't hearing them. With nonfiction it's important to hear the sensibility and persona of the writer. Read short essays like "Living Like Weasels" by Annie Dillard and "Northeast Direct" by Dagoberto Gilb or the opening chapters of *The Diving Bell and the Butterfly* by Jean-Dominique Bauby and you'll hear what I mean.

Writers should also read their own prose aloud. Inevitably you hear things about the rhythm and the sense of the sentences that you don't pick up visually on the page—sometimes it's merely something minor but often it's something that would stall or derail a reader. If you do it aloud often enough, you'll end up doing it automatically but silently when you read a passage over—you'll hear it in your head. That's writing by ear too.

Another way to learn how to write by ear is to examine the structure of sentences. One way to do that is to rearrange them and accentuate their elements by looking at the levels within them. Here's an example of what I mean. Take the passage about the Polyphemus moth by Annie Dillard; arrange each sentence so that it has a separate line starting at the left-hand margin; arrange elements of sentences set off by commas or dashes or parentheses or prepositions under the main clause (or above, if that's where they appear). Here's what you'd get:

> The bell rang twice;
> I had to go.
> The moth was receding down the driveway,
> > > dragging on.
> I went;
> I ran inside.
> The Polyphemus moth is still crawling down the driveway,
> > crawling down the driveway hunched,
> > crawling down the driveway on six
> > > furred feet,
> > > > forever.

Arranged in this fashion you can see the relationships among the sentences and the relationships among the parts of sentences more clearly. The method of Dillard's text becomes more obvious.

Or take the concluding sentence of White's passage from "Songbirds":

> And in the east
> > beyond the lilac and
> > beyond the barn and
> > beyond the bay and
> > behind the deepening hills,
> > > in slow and splendid surprise,
> > > > rises the bomber's moon.

I could easily put "rises the bomber's moon" against the left margin because it is the main clause of the sentence but I'm putting it over to the right because it clarifies for me the flow of the sentence, the way those prepositional phrases forestall the main clause and the reversed order of the sentence holds off the final revelation of the subject.

The point of the exercise is not to devise some absolute scheme and develop it into a fetish, as diagramming sentences once became, but rather to tinker with a process for looking at sentences in a different way than we usually read them on the page and discovering something about the way they go together. You miss things in silent reading of traditional paragraphs, things you miss even in oral reading, that this approach highlights. When you use it on your own prose, it draws your attention to your own (often inadvertent) devices, the way your sentences may frequently be the same length or the same structure or produce unintentional echoes in repetitions of words and phrases or misdirect the reader away from the things you want to emphasize. White's sentence above would be perfectly acceptable but entirely different in emphasis if it read:

> And, in slow and splendid surprise,
> the bomber's moon rises in the east
>   beyond the lilac,
>   the barn,
>   the bay, and
>   the deepening hills.

The sentence is now leading us away, off into the distance, toward "the deepening hills," instead of zooming slowly out of the farmyard past, in turn, the lilac, the barn, the bay, and the deepening hills in order to focus our attention on the ominous brightness of "the bomber's moon." I have no evidence of how White arrived at the sentence he did publish, but it wouldn't be unusual for him to have moved the parts of one version of the sentence around until he found one that fit the mood, the tone, the attitude of the moment and ended the piece in a way he thought would have the right kind of impact.

In the same way you can see how deliberate Annie Dillard's intentions were in the Polyphemus moth passage when you attempt to revise it for less repetition and more directness:

> The bell rang twice;
> I had to go,
>   running inside
>   while the receding moth was dragging on down the driveway.

The hunched Polyphemus moth is still forever crawling on six furred feet down the driveway.

What a loss is here in this revision. Eliminating repetition, shifting word order, I am able to retain the words of the passage but lose entirely their original feeling, their sensibility; I have diminished the passage simply by reducing its meaning to its actions and erasing its emotional impact, the reflection that resonated from its design.

You can see this kind of thing happen in your own prose by taking a paragraph, arranging the sentences by levels around the main clause, and then tinkering with that structure by changing word order, shifting the relationships among sentences and parts of sentences, and breaking up and recombining sentences and clauses and phrases. Try rewriting the passage in the fewest number of words that will get the same ideas across (I once wrote television reviews for a weekly contest in a local newspaper, my first drafts usually 200–300 words long but my final drafts of necessity only 150 words long—a nifty challenge in concision and control of language). Try rewriting the passage in the fewest number of sentences (see if you can make six sentences into three or two or one). Try shuffling around the order of the sentences, making the middle one first, the first one last, and so on. Then look at the variations altogether and ask yourself which combination works best for your purposes, what differences the variations make in the meaning, the sense, the impact of the original language and the fundamental ideas. Read the variations aloud, listening to the rhythms, the pace, the sounds of the words in relationship to one another.

The least that can happen with this exercise is that you'll recognize how many options you have with your prose. The best will be that you begin to develop or further develop your awareness of the melodies, the harmonies, the sympathetic tuning in your language. You'll better appreciate the possibilities of writing by ear.

10

PLACE

Place isn't only a destination; it's also a threshold through which to enter time and text. Where we dwell influences who we are as individuals—it's the impulse to memoir and personal essay; where we venture reveals who we are as observers—it's the impulse to travel and nature narrative and reportage; where we go in the paths of others tells us who we are as readers—it's the impulse to cultural criticism. Does it make a difference that Alfred Kazin (*A Walker in the City*) grew up in Brownsville instead of Bensonhurst, where Marianna Torgovnick (*Crossing Ocean Parkway*) did, or Sacramento, where Joan Didion (*Where I Was From*) did, or Pittsburgh, where Annie Dillard (*An American Childhood*) did? Does it make a difference that E. B. White (*One Man's Meat*) lived on a saltwater farm on the coast of Maine, instead of in Dakota, where Kathleen Norris (*Dakota*) did, or Wyoming, where Gretel Ehrlich (*The Solace of Open Spaces*) did, or Denver, where Robert Michael Pyle (*The Thunder Tree*) did? Does it make a difference that Patricia Hampl's grandmother came from Czechoslovakia (*A Romantic Education*) and Richard Rodriguez's parents came from Mexico (*Hunger of Memory*), that Judith Cofer's parents came from Puerto Rico (*Silent Dancing*) and Naomi Shihab Nye's parents came from

Palestine (*Never in a Hurry*)? Only someone with no concept of rhetorical questions would pause before answering "Yes" to all of the above. Where we are and where we come from and where we've been—in a word, *place*—is a defining part of who we are and what our lives and our experiences have been. It's surely a part of fiction—think of Faulkner, Joyce, Proust, and Woolf. It's a part of poetry—think of Frost, Whitman, Dickinson, and Jeffers. It's a part of drama—think of Tennessee Williams and Eugene O'Neill. And it's surely a part of nonfiction in all its forms. Place is vital and central—integral—to our lives and, consequently, to the writing we do about them.

I wanted to know more about composing the nonfiction of place. When I wrote essays of place—about Mesa Verde and Chaco Canyon, about the Bitterroot Mountains, about the shorelines of the Great Lakes—I composed mostly from innate knowledge; that is, I drew upon direct experience of place and the intuitions of a habitual writer and reader. I hadn't examined how my own essays or those I read by others functioned as evocations of place. Instinct and experience worked well enough, most of the time, but the nonfiction writer in me craved a deeper awareness of what happened in my own composing and the nonfiction theorist in me wanted a more concrete knowledge of what strategies other writers had used or might use. So I devised an interactive project for myself: To see what I could glean as a reader, I decided to examine some well-established and highly accomplished examples of the nonfiction of place, works that I believed achieved whatever it is one achieves in the form; to see what I could glean as a writer, I decided to compose an essay about a place I had not written about before, one I knew little or nothing about, in order to observe how I came to terms with the place.

I think this is the way nonfiction writing begins—with a vague curiosity, an unarticulated suspicion, of which the writer is hardly aware (how many similar questions or suspicions evaporate unrecognized, unacknowledged, unremembered?) but which somehow takes strong enough root in the imagination to impel the writer onto the path to (or *into* the path *of*) some sort of resolution. That quest is nourished by an inchoate optimism—we expect that putting ourselves in an environment that sustains our curiosity will allow our desires to achieve fruition. Something will come of this, we think, perhaps something worth remembering, worth preserving, worth sharing. Our thoughts and experiences, as they register in the brain, automatically kick open synapses leading to other thoughts and experiences suspended in memory; because they do, something inevitably *does* come of this, something unique to the writer. It requires only a commitment or an exercise of will, traceable to who knows what source, to flower fully.

Following my own trail of open synapses I quickly began reflecting on Great Pond, in Maine, the setting for E. B. White's essay "Once More to the Lake." I happened to know a great deal about how White had come to write that essay in 1941, was certain that the resort camp where he and his son had stayed was still open, but had never been to the actual site. If I wrote about that unfamiliar location, I calculated, I might better understand how White composed his own nonfiction of place. As I mulled over this possibility, further associative links opened. I began to consider Walden Pond, in Massachusetts, the site of Henry David Thoreau's great book and a location that would give me over a hundred and fifty years of perspective. Eventually I talked myself into visiting both Great Pond and Walden Pond and writing an essay (or two) about both locations. This scheme offered me rich possibilities for comparative experiences as both a reader and a writer, and it also promised to open circuits between the reading and the writing.

I didn't realize it at the time, but the places I had decided to write about were already beginning to shape the nonfiction I *would* write. This is also the way nonfiction works—the writing emerges from the subject as the writer tries to make sense of it. For example, after my on-site research and avid journalizing at Great Pond I remembered that White had written an essay on Walden; I reread it at once and suddenly found myself, as I drove toward Concord, traveling with the spirit of that text as a passenger. In some ways the writer's job is to keep up with the writing, to discover the form *it* needs to take, the direction *it* needs to go.

To complete my project on the nonfiction of place I reread "Once More to the Lake" and *Walden*, went to Great Pond and visited

White's grave in Maine, reread White's essay "Walden," and went to Walden Pond and visited Thoreau's grave in Concord. I wrote about my reading and my wandering in my daybook, on-site at ponds and cemeteries, and in my journal, in rented rooms and libraries and cafés and restaurants. I returned home to Michigan, transcribed my daybook and journal entries into computer files and drafted, revised, and eventually completed two interlinked essays. I wanted readers to visit those sites in two or three different periods, through excerpts from texts by Thoreau and White imbedded within mine, and to compare the landscapes as each of us saw them and portrayed them. It took a certain amount of naïveté or chutzpah—or possibly folly—to juxtapose my prose with theirs, but it was necessary if the essays were to establish or generate place for their readers just as they re-create or recover place for me.

In the end the project led me, both as a reader and as a writer, to a richer and more complex understanding of place in nonfiction. For one thing, it helped me determine the range and variety of works that belong to what may be termed as "the nonfiction of place."

※

Place is a significant element in nonfiction, sometimes secondary, sometimes primary. Traditionally, going back at least as far as Aristotle's "Poetics," setting has been one of the essentials of literature, along with theme, character, plot, diction, and thought. In the nonfiction of place, the landscape of the work, the backdrop against which events take place, is often foregrounded to such an extent that it is the primary focus of the work. It is central to the meaning or impact of the work. For readers familiar with the locale, the presentation of place is successful if they recognize the accuracy and insight of the re-creation; that is, no matter how they react to the essayist's interpretation of life in that setting, they should still be able to say, "Yes, I know this place; this account is true to the place where I live." At the same time readers unfamiliar with the setting gain a sense of having been there, of having occupied or experienced that textual place. Readers of nature and travel narratives, in particular, hope for a sense of having lived in a space they have never inhabited. In the most successful nonfiction of place, both kinds of readers, insiders and outsiders, feel they are in the same space, feel they would know the space again if they visited it in person. Most literary works are enhanced by a sense of specific space. Most readers want to know where they're supposed to be in their reading—or for that matter, in their viewing. Films that are set in generic cities or countrysides are less compelling than those set in a specific time and place. In all literature, setting at least establishes a context for events, influences to some degree how we perceive what we encounter.

In the nonfiction of place in particular, setting has such an impact upon characters or events or atmosphere that specific place is inextricable from everything else in the work—the story cannot be transposed casually from one setting to another; the narrator cannot be easily confused with someone from a different part of the country; the events cannot be imagined as being enacted elsewhere. The nonfiction of place is never about generic locations, never set everywhere and nowhere. For me at least, the danger inherent in travel narratives where the author passes through some potentially fascinating terrain will be the difficulty of making the landscape come alive; if I get deep into the book, or, less likely, finish it, and still have no feeling that I've been there—or worse, that the author has been there—the book is a failure for me. For example, any number of books have followed routes of pilgrimage—to Santiago de Compostela in Spain, say, or Canterbury in England—but the success of the book will hinge on how fully both author and reader feel a sense of place, a sense of why the pilgrimage is worth making.

The literary works that make up the nonfiction of place include flat-out, up-front explorations of particular locales, pilgrimages to special sites, tours of specific terrain, narratives of travel or residence or investigation—indeed, any nonfiction form in which the reader comes away with a powerful sense of place, a vicarious sense of having been there, perhaps in addition to whatever else the book provides. The nonfiction of place, then, encompasses any number of subgenres and forms. It can be an essay like E. B. White's "Once More to the Lake," recounting a visit the author makes with his son to the

Maine camp where he stayed with his family as a child, or Scott Russell Sanders's "Cloud Crossing," telling of the author's hike up an Oregon mountain with his infant son; it can be a memoir like *Christ Stopped in Eboli* by Carlo Levi, a record of his internal exile to a remote region of Italy during Mussolini's regime and his discovery of its landscape and its people's lives, or *All but the Waltz* by Mary Clearman Blew, collecting essays about family history that are also recreations of life in Montana; it can be a travel narrative like Robert Louis Stevenson's *Travels with a Donkey in the Cévennes*, one of the classic walking stories, or André Aciman's "In Search of Proust," about visiting the town upon which Proust's novels are based; it can be a scientific meditation like Chet Raymo's "Celebrating Creation," about watching the Northern Lights and pondering scientific and religious ideas of creation at the Gallus Oratory in Ireland, or Diane Ackerman's "White Lanterns," studying penguins in Antarctica; it can be literary reportage like John McPhee's "The Search for Marvin Gardens," tracing elements of the game of Monopoly through the streets of Atlantic City, or Susan Orlean's *The Orchid Thief*, set in the backwaters of the Everglades; it can be a nature narrative like *The Outermost House* by Henry Beston, the classic account of a year spent on the beach on Cape Cod, or *This Cold Heaven* by Gretel Ehrlich, recounting her immersion in the landscape of Greenland. When we recognize how important place is to such various works, we realize that place is a vital element of nonfiction.

⚬⚬⚬

Writers approach place, generally speaking, from the perspective of either an insider or an outsider. The insider's story is often about observation, a narrative of close examination of landscape and locale expressing what time and repetition of experience teach the dweller about place. The outsider's story is often about discovery, a narrative of entering into landscape and locale and learning either how the sojourner passes through it or how to become a dweller in it oneself. The insider is an inhabitant, a denizen, a dweller; the outsider is a transient, a traveler, an interloper (in the sense of one *loping*—or striding—*through* unfamiliar terrain). The inhabitant's advantage is the ability to let understanding accumulate, to have unasked questions answered almost by osmosis rather than by confrontation or direct investigation; he or she has rehearsed the explanation of experience by thinking or talking about it over time, so that the words that emerge in the writing about place come from a deep, broad pool of familiarity. The interloper's advantage is to be able to see things afresh, to ask questions that the inhabitant doesn't think to ask because the answers are so familiar as to become transparent; he or she draws instinctively on experiences of other places in order to understand the one under consideration, so that the words that emerge in the writing surface insights prompted by conscientious scrutiny and candid questioning. Both intimacy and distance have advantages.

Thoreau wrote about Walden Pond as an inhabitant. He built a cabin a little distance from the pond, lived there two years, and kept a journal that served as a major resource for the early draft of *Walden*. His inhabitant position came spontaneously from being in place for so long—growing up in Concord, he had visited the pond often and he continued to tramp around it for years after he lived there—but without his habit of close observation and thoughtful, prolific journalizing he might not have been able to represent that inhabitant position in his text.

Thoreau was relentlessly observant as well as thoroughly experienced in the space he moved through. He had a great deal of stored knowledge, both collected and innate, to draw on in his writing about the pond. *Walden* is permeated by his sense of place, in part because his sense of place permeates him. For example, Thoreau reveals his feeling for place in his vivid account of an evening walk:

> This is a delicious evening, when the whole body is one sense, and imbibes delight through every pore. I go and come with a strange liberty in Nature, a part of herself. As I walk along the stony shore of the pond in my shirt sleeves, though it is cool as well as cloudy and windy, and I see nothing special to attract me, all the elements are unusually congenial to me. The bullfrogs trump to usher in the night, and the note of the whippoorwill is borne on the rippling wind from over the water.

The passage, written in the lyrical or simultaneous present tense, establishes a sensation of place, the feeling that is excited in someone by moving through this particular terrain. It gives us the idea that the writer has been (or at the moment both of his writing and our reading actually is) in this location.

In other passages Thoreau writes with the scientific detachment of a surveyor and naturalist. For example, he describes the pond as "a clear and deep green well, half a mile long and a mile and three quarters in circumference, and contains about sixty-one-and-a-half acres; a perennial spring in the midst of pine and oak woods, without any visible inlet or outlet except by the clouds and evaporation." In a later chapter he includes a map of the pond complete with locations for depth soundings, and measurements of area, circumference, and length.

Thoreau's depth of familiarity with the place as well as his thoroughness of observation emerges most clearly in those passages where he reveals the various angles and seasons of his viewing. At one point he writes: "Walden is blue at one time and green at another, even from the same point of view. . . . Viewed from a hill-top it reflects the color of the sky, but near at hand it is of a yellowish tint next the shore where you can see the sand, then a light green, which gradually deepens to a uniform dark green in the body of the pond." This conscientious, thorough examination extends to a number of details that the casual visitor to the pond might easily overlook or observe without particular notice or curiosity. In talking about the paths around the pond, Thoreau not only notes their presence but also reflects on their origins:

> I have been surprised to detect encircling the pond, even where a thick wood has just been cut down on the shore, a narrow shelf-like path in the steep hill-side, alternately rising and falling, approaching and receding from the water's edge, as old probably as the race of man here, worn by the feet of aboriginal hunters, and still from time to time unwittingly trodden by the present occupants of the land. This is particularly distinct to one standing on the middle of the pond in winter, just after a light snow has fallen, appearing as a clear undulating white line, unobscured by weeds and twigs a quarter of a mile off in many places where in summer it is hardly distinguishable

close at hand. The snow reprints it, as it were, in clear white type alto-relievo.

The comparison at the close of the passage makes the image come alive for a reader, but only someone who has been repeatedly in a certain locale would begin to distinguish features such as this. Thoreau brings to his description of the pond not only his skills as a naturalist and a surveyor but also the advantage of long association with place. Dwelling in his native ground is not only his motive for making sense of it but also his means. Granted, *Walden* is not simply about physical place or about natural history in a specific locale; nonetheless, on a certain level it could be said to be about developing an intensive sensitivity to place. A sense of place suffuses the entire book, perhaps because a sense of place suffuses the writer.

This may—in fact I'm sure it does—explain how E. B. White was able to create the sense of place that permeates his essay "Once More to the Lake." He was not a long-time resident of the Maine camp but he had the advantage of frequent, recurring, intensive occupancies for short periods over a thirty-six-year period. He was perhaps technically a transient in that environment but he was no casual passer-through. He had begun coming to the lake as a five-year-old and was forty-two when he wrote the essay, having written about it frequently over the years in pretend brochures, letters, and journal entries. When he came to write the essay he had already rehearsed its themes and his responses to his experiences there on a number of other occasions. Perhaps, in addition to its affecting power, what contributes greatly to the sense of place that underlies the essay is its aura of lived experience, its simultaneous superimposition of place and persona on the page. In the nonfiction of place the author's persona is not simply situated in place; more compellingly, place is situated within—and emerges from—the author.

⸺ ⟡ ⸺

I tend to write not as an inhabitant but as an interloper. As an essayist of place I'm not even remotely a travel writer—that is, I don't visit places in order to write about them and pave the way for my potential readers to visit such places; I write about places as a way of remembering and responding to and reflecting upon the ones that somehow affect me, that move me to write about them. Writing on-site—sitting on a mountain ledge looking across a valley, sitting on a dune looking across a beach, sitting on a remnant of a wall looking at an expanse of ruins—makes me pay more attention to what I'm looking at, locks it more firmly in memory; writing later in my journal about what I thought or felt at the site often brings to the surface associations only I can make, juxtapositions that arise because they happen to be stored in my memory or be part of my experience. Sometimes a writer's reflections run parallel to thoughts other writers have had and may be valuable because they confirm a common thread of connection to a place; sometimes, perhaps more often, a writer's reflections are idiosyncratic, unique to the writer, and valuable precisely because they raise our awareness of other ways of looking at a specific locale.

In an essay titled "Cahokia," about the prehistoric mounds across the Mississippi River from St. Louis, Elizabeth Dodd not only helps the reader to imagine what this archaeological site looks like, but also links the life that scientists and historians believe was lived there with the life she sees around her as a sojourner in St. Louis. She relies in part on powers of description generated by close observance of her unfamiliar surroundings. In the essay she explains that, after her teaching job in Kansas has ended for the semester, she is rejoining her husband to spend the summer in St. Louis, where he is still in graduate school.

Here we have no air-conditioning, no laundry facilities in the apartment. A grid of clotheslines crisscrosses the cement plaza at the building's rear and today I carried wet clothes there from the washer in the basement, passing up the single drier in the windowless, musty room to the ample space out back, although I met no one else while at my work. It was a small act, a tiny one, not really geared to reattach life to—well, to what, really? It was a splendid day.

But after the laundry dried, after the lights began to come on in the stairwells of the facing building, I sat on this apartment's small balcony to watch the night fall. Chimney swifts chattered overhead, the jet planes roared from distance to distance, and at last a woman across the way came out to read the evening paper before the daylight disappeared. All around, the life of the comfortable city continued its background noise, and farther away, the more desperate lives in East St. Louis continued well out of sight and hearing.

Dodd evokes place by calling upon what she sees and what she reacts to in her new surroundings. At Cahokia her activities exploring the mounds lead her to reflect on her position in both time and place.

To stand atop this earthen structure today is still an exhilarating event although not a terrifying one. For people living in the Mississippi area almost 1,000 years ago, it might have been both. Tallgrasses—mostly switchgrass—riffle in the wind, and the sounds of traffic on the interstate to the north and the state route to the south both shift in tone, a sort of slow, subtle Doppler effect as one rises from the floodplain.

On a clear, warm day, breathing deeply from the 154-step climb, I'm alone on the artificial, nearly level summit. Distance becomes enticing, interesting in its new perspective. To the west, the tall buildings and Gateway Arch of downtown St. Louis look like a model city, the architect's miniature on display. Nearer, the clusters of mounds rise from the flat prairie in a seemingly scattered pattern. Of the original 120 mounds, 68 remain, nestled amid homes and highways—and recent, failed symbols of twentieth-century life. One mound was demolished in the 1950s in order to erect a drive-in theater. In Collinsville the drive-in has fared no better than it has elsewhere. . . .

What she sees influences what she reflects upon; she doesn't have layers of personal prehistory in this place to draw on or to divert her attention from physical details. In order to have a sense of place about an unfamiliar locale, the writer has to ask herself, "What am I seeing? What does it mean? Why do I react to it the way I do?"

The drive to Cahokia, across the Mississippi from St. Louis, takes her through the poverty and decay of East St. Louis and when she considers the population density and cruel social customs of the ancient mound dwellers—their rulers were buried with slaves and mass graves reveal brutal atrocities—she finds comparisons with the degradations of modern American urban life unavoidable. The contrast between the prehistoric world and the modern world may be there for any visitor to see, but not every writer would make those associations. But the essay isn't only pointing out inequality and injustice across millennia; the author also hints at similar, more intimate versions of these issues in her own crumbling marriage. This is the way that writing about place uncovers intersections of social and personal and natural history across time, and confronts the writer not only with what she observes but also with who she is.

An interloper writing nonfiction about a place is as obligated as an inhabitant to write honestly about whatever he or she observes, but unlike the dweller, the transient makes no claim the views presented weren't collected in passing. The reader is obligated to accept those conditions for considering place—all of us, whether we write or we don't, experience place both as inhabitants and as interlopers. We ought to be able to acknowledge the credibility and vitality of either perspective.

—————— ∞∞∞ ——————

If the poles of perspective for the nonfiction of place are occupied at one extreme by denizens and at the other by drifters, it's obvious that there are a multitude of sites in between, innumerable intersections of longitude and latitude where others situate themselves—those who stay in a place long enough to become acclimated beyond the casual but not long enough to feel thoroughly intimate. No one writer necessarily occupies just one site throughout his or her career. Thoreau, the *über*-inhabitant of Walden Pond, was an interloper in his writings published posthumously as *The Maine Woods, Cape Cod,* and *A Yankee in Canada.* E. B. White, the insider writing about life on a saltwater farm in "The Flocks We Watch by Night" and "Death of a Pig," also often took on the role of outsider in his essays; in "The World of Tomorrow," he visits the 1939 New York World's Fair like any other attendee, reports on what he sees and does, and reflects on what he feels and how he responds; in "The Ring of Time," especially the great opening segment in a Sarasota circus tent, he portrays himself a bystander, a mere vacationer in Florida, observing life in the south from the perspective of a New England Yankee. His persona in either essay is that of an outsider; he never pretends to an insider's perspective.

Perhaps some of this is simply unavoidable. If we write about a place we know we almost can't help conjuring contexts that affect how we perceive the location; if we write about a place we are encountering for the first time, we almost can't help dwelling on direct observation and the associations and reactions they produce. Our longitude and latitude may be determined by our relative distance from each of the two poles of perspective.

However, on many of those intersections are transients traveling while immersed in texts by earlier inhabitants and interlopers. They not only see place directly, as those other writers do, but simultaneously view it through an additional lens, a textual prism. If we write about a place familiar to us from our reading, our vision is refracted—our response influenced—by the earlier writing; we see the place principally in terms of how it compares in reality (that is, how it appears to us at the moment we encounter it) to the way it appears in another writer's text.

This is not an uncommon approach to the nonfiction of place; witness the number of books retracing the routes of Lewis and Clark in the American West or Johnson and Boswell through Scotland to the Hebrides; witness Richard Holmes (in *Footsteps*) traveling without a donkey through the Cévennes on the trail of Robert Louis Stevenson or John McPhee (in *Pieces of the Frame*) making his reading of *Macbeth* concrete by walking with his family from Birnam Wood to Dunsinane or Ann Zwinger and Edwin Way Teale (in *A Conscious Stillness*) replicating the journey of Henry Thoreau and his brother down the Concord and Merrimack Rivers. Such an approach presents a portrait of place through a translucent scrim that changes, with the intensity of the lighting, from nearly invisible and transparent to wholly visible and solid, like those two-way mirrors which, with a twist of a dial, superimpose the image of your face onto the face of the person on the other side of the glass. We seem to occupy two (or more) different compass points at once.

A good example is E. B. White's essay "Walden." White had been writing a monthly column for *Harper's Magazine*, sometimes focusing on quotidian events in his part of Maine, sometimes ranging widely to report on happenings he observed elsewhere. On the occasion of his visit to Concord he cast the essay as a letter to Thoreau himself. It begins: "Miss Nims, take a letter to Henry David Thoreau. Dear Henry: . . ." The essay often alludes to phrases of Thoreau's as it recounts White's wandering around the town and out to the pond and the site of Thoreau's cabin. Early on, describing his approach on the highway, White writes:

> . . . I began to rouse myself from the stupefaction a day's motor journey induces. It was a delicious evening, Henry, when the whole body is one sense and imbibes delight through every pore, if I may coin a phrase. Fields were richly brown where the harrow, drawn by the stripped Ford, had lately sunk its teeth; pastures were green; and overhead the sky had that same everlasting great look that you will find on page 144 of the Oxford pocket edition. I could feel the road entering me, through tire, wheel, spring, and cushion; shall I not have intelligence with earth too? Am I not partly leaves and vegetable mold myself?–a man of infinite horsepower, yet partly leaves.

The second sentence in the passage repeats a familiar sentence of Thoreau's that I quoted earlier in this chapter. Even if we don't know the specific allusion here or in White's last lines, we suspect he's paraphrasing or quoting Thoreau. In the second case, the reference is to a scene where (on page 138 of the Princeton edition) Thoreau, imagining nature in sympathy "if any man should ever for a just cause grieve," asks, "Shall I not have intelligence with the earth? Am I not partly leaves and vegetable mold myself?'" This constant hearkening back to *Walden* gives us some perspective on the sights that White records. Later he tells Henry (or us):

> The evening was full of sounds, some of which would have stirred your memory. The robins still love the elms of New England villages at sundown. There is enough of the thrush in them to make song inevitable at the end of day, and enough of the tramp to make them hang round the dwellings of men.

Description comes into the essay as both a reminder to "Henry" of what the village was like and an update on what it is like now.

The contrast between then and now runs through the essay, as well as a sometimes implicit, sometimes explicit contrast between Thoreau and White. White is constantly aware of how typically twentieth-century-American Concord has become and how he himself has a different sensibility from Thoreau's, no matter how much in sympathy with the earlier writer he may be. For example, he explains such mundane activities as locking his car doors to protect the laprobe, notes that the highway has a "cotton surface," and comments on the sound of "Amos and Andy" on the radio. When he walks out to the pond he writes:

> I knew I must be nearing your woodland retreat when the Golden Pheasant lunchroom came into view—Sealtest ice cream, toasted sandwiches, hot frankfurters, waffles, tonics, and lunches. Were I the proprietor, I should add rice, Indian meal, and molasses—just for old time's sake.

By the end of the essay readers have a thorough impression of the kind of town Concord has evolved into as well as ways White sees himself as falling somewhat short of living up to Thoreau's example. If we were to take out the overt references to Thoreau in White's essay, we'd find that the piece loses much of its point and punch and all of its implications about change in a place over time. It would also take away all of Concord's resonance as a historic or literary site.

Even works that don't expressly follow in another writer's footsteps display echoes and reflections of earlier writing, other investigations, literary influences and factual resources. These ingredients give essays of place distinctive flavors, according to how they're mixed. Some are more lyrical or more narrative or more expository because of the mix; some border on poetry, some on science; some are such a jumble of motives and modes and intentions and conventions that only vague terms like "creative nonfiction" or "the nonfiction of place" are sufficiently encompassing. As Deborah Tall has noted, "Books about places are so often adventurous hybrids in which physical description, character portraits, statistics, analysis, personal narrative, dramatic event, argument, meditation, and flights of fancy can happily coexist. Books of place are geographical, ethnographic, environmental, political, spiritual." This truth about the nonfiction of place helps explain why its titles are shelved and scattered throughout bookstores and libraries rather than handily grouped in one location.

Some nonfiction works are expressly and explicitly essays of place; they set out to explore and to understand certain terrain. Other nonfiction works are only incidentally and implicitly essays of place; they set out to tell a story of a life experience or report events of one kind or another and in order to fully accomplish what they set out to do must also fully present place. For Elizabeth Arthur to tell the story of her and her husband's retreat to solitude and its devastating effect on their marriage, she has to make the setting vivid in *Island Sojourn*; for Jon Krakauer to tell the story of how one young man's dream of living a simple life went terribly wrong, he has to place the reader in the setting where the young man died, in *Into the Wild*; for John Calderazzo to make us understand the nature of volcanoes, he must locate them in their geological and geographical contexts in *Rising Fire*; for Michael Gorra to explain the conflict between German history and the conventions of travel literature, he must make specific sites in Germany come alive for us in *The Bells in Their Silence*. These works may be classified, respectively, as memoir, literary journalism, science narrative, and travel/cultural criticism, but all blend place seamlessly into their designs.

Readers find empathy or understanding in an honest story but nonetheless need to know where they are. Writers can't generate a sense of place in readers until they've generated a sense of place in themselves and find a way to project it onto the page. Those who do it most successfully, no matter what else their writing may also be, will have contributed to the nonfiction of place.

NOTES FOR NONFICTIONISTS: PLACE

So how might we write a nonfiction of place? A nonfiction of place arises from a writer's immersion in a particular landscape. One way to do that is by *exploring familiar terrain*, discovering all we know about the place, and making that knowledge understandable to readers; another way is by *exploring unfamiliar terrain*, recording what we discover about the place, and making our discoveries capable of being lived by readers; a third way is by *exploring terrain across time* in the company of an earlier writer, comprehending the influences that time and perspective have in the way we perceive a place, and creating the means for readers to comprehend them as well. These approaches correspond to the perspectives writers have on place.

The inhabitant perspective draws on the experience of dwelling in a certain landscape or locale. It's good to see how other writers have handled similar terrain; reading Thoreau's *Walden* has inspired any number of writers to do a similar deep dwelling on their own particular landscape. In *Ceremonial Time*, for example, John Hanson Mitchell has written thoroughly about Scratch Flat, a square mile of land on which he lived in Massachusetts, trying to trace the history of this patch of ground not only through his habitation of it but all the way back to its formation. Sue Hubbell follows the seasons in *A Country Year: Living the Questions*, set in the Ozarks; Edward Abbey's classic *Desert Solitaire: A Season in the Wilderness* is set in Arches National Park; Chet Raymo's *The Path: A One-Mile Walk through the Universe* is a deep history of his route from home to work; Terry Tempest Williams in *Refuge*, Annie Dillard in *Pilgrim at Tinker Creek*, Deborah Tall in *From Where We Stand* all set out to thoroughly explore a plot of terrain where they live; John Daniel, in *Rogue River Journal: A Winter Alone* and Barbara J. Scot in *The Stations of Still Creek* both explore solitude in place. The urban answer to *Walden* may be Alfred Kazin's *A Walker in the City*, not only a great American memoir of growing up Jewish in the 1920s but also a vivid evocation of New York City recreating an era; like Thoreau in Concord Kazin is continually sauntering through the neighborhoods of his childhood, bringing the personal past and its particular milieu back to life, and modeling another way that an inhabitant can write a nonfiction of place.

To capture an inhabitant's perspective, the writer needs to examine the sites of experience. A physical visit is an obvious approach. While researching a memoir of my childhood I retraced familiar routes I took to school or to downtown or to friends' houses and was amazed at the memories and images that surfaced out of the past, bringing back scenes I thought I'd forgotten. The visit in place not only recovers experience but also gives you an opportunity to check specific details of landscape and architecture. To better anchor your discoveries in memory, tours of this kind would benefit from walking with a tape recorder, taking fieldnotes on-site, and/or writing journal entries immediately afterwards.

In addition—or as an alternative—to an actual physical visit, it is also possible to take a tour imaginatively—in effect, a virtual tour—through visual images or guided imagery.

To make a visual visit you need old photographs or films or videotapes. With images it's possible not simply to describe what you see in your hand but to use a combination of memory and imagination to enter the photograph and snoop around. Don't merely look at the people at the center of the frame; look over their shoulders at the background and then try to reconstruct the setting. With enough concentration, you can step into the photograph and take a good look around, even to see what the people in the picture were looking at beyond the photographer. The writing you do out of this visit attempts to capture the feeling of having been in the photograph or on-site when the photograph was taken.

To make a psychological visit, you have to imagine yourself walking through familiar terrains, using a kind of self-guided imagery—you close your eyes and try to picture what you saw when you moved through this landscape in the past. A couple of easy examples: Close your eyes, then imagine yourself opening your eyes in your bedroom on a typical childhood morning—look around you at the familiar setting and take in what you see, then get out of bed and be the subjective camera eye moving through the house in your familiar routine. Or imagine yourself opening your eyes as you enter your school building—follow your gaze as you walk through the halls and notice the people around you and head for your locker or your classroom, even accompany yourself through your course schedule and revisit all your classes and teachers. Or use a photograph as a starting point—a picture of a room in a house or a building on a street in a town or a trailhead in the wilderness can be a way into a psychological tour of the entire setting. Describe what you see in these visits, in logs or journals or drafts, in such a way that a reader would be able to see what you saw.

These approaches are ways of getting into place, particularly getting into place when you're not actually in place. The reliable old-fashioned way is to write about place while you're in place. Thoreau is our great example of someone who kept a journal of what he noticed and encountered in his daily ambles around his home terrain, recording details and discoveries that he returned to and enlarged upon in drafts of books and essays. The daily journal of observations not only records what the writer sees but also trains the writer to observe more closely, to be more spontaneously observant; it also rehearses the language the writer will use as the basis of drafts and revision. On-site writing is especially important to anyone writing as an interloper. Vague impressions aren't enough to sustain a sense of place or to give sufficient authority to a description of place to satisfy anyone familiar with the location. The interloper perspective needs to develop and utilize powers of close observation of the unfamiliar, a consistent and continual alertness to surroundings.

One way of training your abilities as an observer is to take your journal or daybook into unfamiliar terrain and begin recording what you see. For example, pick a locale you're unfamiliar with—a museum, a neighborhood, a park, a store—walk through it carefully, and after you come out write about the experience, trying to re-create in your journal what your visit was like. A couple of days later reread that entry, see if you recall things that didn't get into the entry or if your first impressions have been altered by time, then return to the locale and walk through it carefully again. This time look for what you might have missed, trying to discover the significance of your having overlooked or dismissed or avoided certain sections. On this walkthrough keep notes on what you're seeing, on the arrangement of its parts, on the relationships among various elements or components. The recurring visits will help you understand your habits of observation and also sharpen them; they will also lead you into a deeper understanding of what you react to about this place and why you react to it. (Notable examples of work generated in this fashion, in addition to Jane Tompkins's "At the Buffalo Bill Museum," and Terry Tempest Williams's *Leap*, are Patricia Hampl's *Blue Arabesque: A Search for the Sublime*, which opens in the Art Institute of Chicago, and two chapters in Michele Morano's *Grammar Lessons*, "Authenticity and Artifice," about the Altamira cave paintings, and "The Impossible Overcome," about Picasso's "Guernica.")

Writers who write often about nature and the environment or about travel and foreign locales need to take in the setting, watch what's happening around them, and record in fieldnotes what they observe. The prolific American naturalist Edwin Way Teale took copious notes whenever he went wandering and made a point of copying and cataloguing the notes when he returned home, so that he was continually accumulating observations that built an expansive sense of place. The deeper and broader his understanding of the terrain about which he wrote, the firmer and more solid the foundation of his writing. In his case fieldnotes produced voluminous background material he could consult and adopt in his later composing, but even without that intention note taking is often productive simply because it helps anchor information in the mind—when the time comes to write, it may not always be necessary to review the notes because the information has become so firmly lodged in the writer's memory—and it also makes the writer better prepared to connect the next day's outing with the one before.

Working from the perspective of an earlier text, entering place through the doorway of another writer's work, alters your perspective on what you're seeing. Some of my favorite books are those in which the writer travels in the company of a book written years, even centuries, before. A brilliant example is *Great Heart: The History of a Labrador Adventure* by James West Davidson and John Rugge. It draws on books, diaries, and journals as well as personal experiences to re-create several epic journeys over the same terrain. Another example is Ivan Doig's *Winter Brothers: A Season at the Edge of America*, a very influential book of this kind for me. In it Doig wanders around the Pacific Northwest while reading and quoting from a diary kept by James Gilchrist Swan a century earlier. The effect on a reader of this kind of work is not unlike a documentary that crosscuts between recent footage of a contemporary explorer with first person voice-over narration and stock footage made up of old still photographs and grainy silent film with actors reciting the words of historical figures. For the writer the effect is like time travel—you watch yourself simultaneously move through the immediate present and shadow another person in the distant past. The experience affects the way you view the terrain you pass through. Everywhere you try to see what the earlier writer might have seen, and the effort makes you more alert to what you actually see, because it gives you some basis of comparison. Once you can tell what's missing and identify what's still there, you've reached the point of comprehending something about the landscape deeper than mere offhand observation.

This kind of experience can be another experiment or training exercise for the writer of place. Simply find a locale in someone else's writing that it would be possible for you yourself to visit in company with that author's prose. Having read about it, how do you imagine the place will be? When you get on-site what do you think is the same or different than you imagined it? Consult the other writer's text and look for whatever might stand out and see what you can find in the landscape that confirms or refutes what's in the prose. What you discover in the landscape that the prose has prepared you for will help you appreciate how the nonfiction of place re-creates terrain for a reader; what you discover in the landscape that hasn't been in the other writer's prose will prepare you to be a sharper observer on your own.

11

TRUTH

Although I don't agree that anyone nowadays can simply define "nonfiction" as "not fiction," I *do* agree with a wide spectrum of writers and writing teachers that, whatever else nonfiction *is*, it definitely *isn't* fiction. Most people who struggle to put limits on creative nonfiction attempt at some point to confine it to fact or reality or veracity or truth. Some people actually refer to it as the "literature of fact" or the "art of truth," and some have even tried to coin terms like "faction" or "realature." Discussions of what is or should be permissible in nonfiction in terms of compressed time periods, combined characters, or invented events take up much space in literary journals and much time at literary conventions. When you toss terms like "the nonfiction novel" and "narrative nonfiction" into the conversation, there's even further confusion. We usually think of a novel as, by definition, fiction, and thus a book like Truman Capote's *In Cold Blood*, the best-known example of a "nonfiction novel," would be a "nonfiction fiction." That would seem to be a contradiction or a paradox, unless you consider narrative to be a mode of discourse and fiction to be a genre which communicates largely through narrative. In that case, though "narrative" and "fiction" may overlap and typically are found in each other's company, they nonetheless are neither synonymous nor coterminous; "novel," then, could indicate only a lengthy narrative form, one usually found in fiction but one capable of being used in nonfiction. It could, but to most people, it doesn't. Though I think we need a good word for a book-length essay as well as one for an essay-length memoir, the term "nonfiction novel" seems to me to have very limited application.

The truth is that every writer has to confront the issue of truth when writing nonfiction. As Annie Dillard has observed, "The elements in any nonfiction should be true not only artistically—the connects must hold at base and must be veracious, for that is the convention and the covenant between the nonfiction writer and his reader." The reason you write nonfiction is to discover the truth about something and to create the most factual rendering of that truth. Or, as Dillard claims, the nonfiction writer "thinks about actual things" and "can make sense of them analytically or artistically."

If, as I've been claiming, "nonfiction is the written expression of, reflection upon, and/or interpretation of observed, perceived, or recollected experience," then it's a literary genre whose ends and means are both truth. The idea of reality or fact is implicit in the definition—"observed experience" refers to something that is happening as the writer records it; "recollected experience" refers to something that happened which the writer later recalls and reports; "perceived experience" refers to something that happened or exists that the writer has found verification for through research, testimony, and deduction confirmed by reliable primary and secondary sources and conscientious consideration of evidence. Note that this assumes on the part of the observer, perceiver, or recollector the honest intention of recording or reporting the truth and, additionally, the capability or capacity to uncover, recognize, and "verify" the truth. (To "verify" means to prove, substantiate, or confirm the "verity"—accuracy or reality—of something.) Even if we exclude from this conversation the willfully deceptive—those who completely fabricate experiences they haven't observed or do not recollect or deliberately mislead readers about what they actually perceive—and even if we accept on good faith the integrity of the observer/perceiver/recollector's efforts, we still can't guarantee the absolute truthfulness of what we read—or for that matter, what we write.

⸺∞⸺

Readers automatically pick up on cues in the writing to determine the factuality of the text. Take, as an example, the following passage from *John James Audubon: The Making of an American*, a biography by Richard Rhodes:

> When Audubon and Joseph Mason arrived at Oakley Plantation on June 18, 1821, they were shown to a cool room on the red-brick ground floor with an outside entrance set back under the jalousied galleries. The large white house above them faced east on grounds shaded by live oaks and magnolias softened by Spanish moss; outside stairs in the rear connected spacious upper floors, with a parlor and a dining room on the second floor and bedrooms on the third. The detached kitchen occupied a separate building behind the house built over the original homestead. Through the summer Oakley would be fully occupied, with James and forty-nine-year-old Lucretia Pirrie in residence; their daughter Eliza, Audubon's pupil; a guest from England, Mrs. Harwood, visiting the Pirries with her little girl; and a friend of Eliza's from New Orleans, Eliza Throgmorton. Mary Ann and Jedediah Smith, Lucretia's daughter by her first marriage and son-in-law, who lived near Oakley on their own plantation, Locust Grove, would be frequent visitors. Almost unmentioned in the contemporary record but present and visible everywhere were the Pirries' several hundred slaves, the engines of their wealth: the Pirries grew cotton.

The passage opens the fourteenth chapter of Rhodes's biography of Audubon, so certain references would be familiar to any attentive reader, but a fact checker assigned to check the facts in this passage would have a great deal to check: not simply the accuracy of the assertion that John James Audubon and Joseph Mason arrived at a certain place on a certain date, but which room they were given, whether the room was shown to them or they were directed to it, a considerable amount of detail about the floor plan, design, and décor of the house in June 1821, the correct names of the individuals residing or visiting there at that date and where they were from, the name of the nearby plantation and the relationship of the owners of it to the owners of Oakley, the source of the Pirries' wealth, and the presence and numbers of slaves. And this is simply the opening paragraph in a chapter less than half way through a book running over four hundred pages long.

A contentious reader might ask, "Well, how can you know all this?"—most readers are not so contentious and take the author's honesty on faith—but an attentive reader has some ideas how Rhodes knows this. For one thing the book has pages and pages of notes, a long bibliography, and acknowledgments identifying a number of individuals in a number of locations who facilitated his research; all these tend to confirm the thoroughness of Rhodes's research. In addition, up to this point in the book Rhodes has quoted often from Audubon's letters, journals, and other manuscripts and published writings. The reader tends to accept the truthfulness of Rhodes's descriptions and declarations and assertions because Rhodes establishes himself as painstakingly thorough at documenting the evidence behind them. Even when at some points the reader might be intuiting interpretations from the evidence presented—for example, the language Audubon uses in connection with one woman he associated with in England while his wife was still in America suggests an attraction that may have led to his at least hoping for a dalliance—Rhodes is cautious: while eventually acknowledging the tone of Audubon's language, he withholds any assertion about the relationship that can't be substantiated by someone's recorded testimony. This kind of caution, which a good many celebrity biographers don't bother to take, builds the reader's confidence in the author's conscientiousness in dealing with his material.

To put it in rhetorical terms, every author creates an ethos or a persona on the page, sometimes openly present in the text, sometimes tactfully transparent, but always a part of the appeal to the reader. As I've suggested before, there's always a writer in the text, whether obvious or indiscernible—"It is always the first person who is speaking," as Thoreau puts it—and the reader accepts the honesty of the author, and the accuracy of the author's text, based in part on an unconscious acceptance of the author's persona and in part on a tendency to trust the sincerity of any author of nonfiction. Only when there's a strong disconnect between the reader's assumptions and the author's assertions do we distrust the author. I'm unlikely to read some writers because they signal a certain bias from the outset (Ann Coulter's titles such as *Treason* and *How to Talk to a Liberal [If You Have To]* and Al Franken's *Lies and the Lying Liars Who Tell Them* both signal a dedication to partisan controversy that I'm not interested in) but I'm more troubled by authors whose agenda is disguised and whose presentation of evidence makes me want to do some fact checking. In part, what I'm driving at is the difficulty of recognizing dishonesty when it's willful and deliberate, instead of either openly ideological or accidental.

Years ago I assigned students to investigate assertions in *Chariots of the Gods?*, Erich von Däniken's best-selling book about the role of extraterrestrials in the development of ancient civilizations. What they and I discovered is the way in which questions von Däniken presented as unanswerable unless aliens were involved—about how the statues on Easter Island were constructed and transported or what the Book of Exodus claimed were the particular properties of the Ark of the Covenant or what certain Mayan pictographs were depicting—had already been answered by reputable scientists, often on the very next page of books from which von Däniken had just quoted. In such books as his, if a reader bothers with them at all, it is necessary to test the assertions of the author, to corroborate or disprove the radical positions being taken; however, unless we're specifically reading in hopes of challenging an author, we tend to expect that nonfiction writers are being honest with us about facts.

But of course not all nonfiction is about the presentation of researched evidence. Much of it is about the experience or the recollection of the author. Read this passage from "Whistling Swan," a section of *Refuge: An Unnatural History of Family and Place* by Terry Tempest Williams:

> Walking the wrackline of Great Salt Lake after a storm is quite different from walking along the seashore after high tide. There are no shells, no popping kelp or crabs. What remains is a bleached narrative

of feathers, bones, occasional birds encrusted in salt and deep piles of brine among the scattered driftwood. There is little human debris among the remote beaches of Great Salt Lake, except for the shotgun shells that wash up after the duck-hunting season.

Yesterday, I walked along the north shore of Stansbury Island. Great Salt Lake mirrored the plumage of immature gulls as they skimmed its surface. It was cold and windy. Small waves hissed each time they broke on shore. Up ahead, I noticed a large, white mound a few feet from where the lake was breaking.

It was a dead swan. Its body lay contorted on the beach like an abandoned lover. I looked at the bird for a long time. There was no blood on its feathers, no sight of gunshot. Most likely, a late migrant from the north slapped silly by a ravenous Great Salt Lake. The swan may have drowned.

I knelt beside the bird, took off my deerskin gloves, and began smoothing feathers. Its body was still limp—the swan had not been dead long. I lifted both wings out from under its belly and spread them on the sand. Untangling the long neck which was wrapped around itself was more difficult, but finally I was able to straighten it, resting the swan's chin flat against the shore.

Beginning with a paragraph generalizing about the shoreline of the lake after a storm, the narrative gives a specific instance when the author explored it at that time and tells how she interacts with what she finds.

A reader here, as with the Audubon biography, might simply take its truthfulness at face value. Unlike the biography, where the persona of Richard Rhodes is off-stage and all is told in third person, here the persona of Terry Tempest Williams is on-stage and events transpire in first person—the author is a character in this memoir, as memoirists tend to be. The narrative is really testimony by an eyewitness and so we accept its reportorial factuality. When she writes a little further on that, "using my own saliva as my mother and grandmother had done to wash my face, I washed the swan's black bill and feet until they shone like patent leather," we may blanch a little at the behavior but don't question its authenticity.

We also more or less accept without challenge the imagery, the use of simile and metaphor: the wrackline is "a bleached narrative," the waves "hissed," the swan's body was "contorted on the beach like an abandoned lover." Metaphor is not a fact; it's an approximation, an equivalence, that generates and is generated by associations. If the swan were contorted like "a water-logged throw rug" or "an elongated pile of cold mashed potatoes" we would think differently about the swan and also about the author's sensitivity to the scene. Generally speaking readers don't challenge a writer's metaphors and comparisons unless they are too jarring or somehow inappropriate.

We can't fact-check metaphors, of course; it would be like challenging the responses to images on a Rorschach test. ("You're wrong; that inkblot doesn't look like two puppies in a hot air balloon, it actually looks like a squid hauling a case of beer.") And readers don't trouble themselves with the "truth" of metaphor. But neither can we fact check the "facts" in this passage—the way the shoreline looks after a storm, the ways the waves sounded to the author or what she saw or whether there was a dead swan and what she did to it. Williams's narrative is no less true than Rhodes's scholarship for being impossible to "verify." As readers we have to take her word for what she saw and did and how it all seemed to her.

Nonfiction depends upon a tacit agreement between writer and reader where the writer will play fair with the facts in exchange for the reader's trust that the writer is sincerely trying to discern and depict truth. The writer can get it wrong, the reader can disagree with the interpretation of evidence, but they are linked by the assumption of an honest effort at verification where possible and a clear signal of uncertainty or imaginative rendering when corroboration is impracticable. About a third of the way through a biographical nonfiction rendering of her title character's life in *Daisy Bates in the Desert*, Julia Blackburn tells us that, although Bates lived for many more years, she left no record of her life whatever such as that the author had drawn on for the first part of the book. When Blackburn then switches gears and writes the remaining two-thirds of the book as a first person narrative in the persona of Daisy Bates, she's writing fiction. Readers may respond differently to this tactic—I for one had been hoping for a wholly nonfictional work—but at least the author has played fair with the reader and signaled the shift. Lauren Slater's

Lying: A Metaphorical Memoir signals its unreliability in its very title and subtitle, though a number of readers, including critics, didn't realize she was not being truthful until they reached the end of the book; I take it that this reaction explains the quote on the cover of the paperback edition: "There is only one kind of memoir I can see to write and that's a slippery, playful, impish, exasperating text, shaped, if it could, like a question mark." Richard Selzer's memoir, *Raising the Dead: A Doctor's Encounter with His Own Mortality*, is even trickier; ostensibly an account of what happened to him while in a coma induced by Legionnaire's disease, it isn't until the end of the book that we realize (Duh!) that the author was in a coma and couldn't possibly have remembered experiencing what he describes—the book is an effort to come to grips with a profound experience that happened while he was unconscious. He writes: "About that death and resurrection? Well, art is a means of acquiring experiences that one never had. Let's leave it at that." It has always been difficult to sort out Selzer's first person short stories from his first person essays, and not all readers will find that conclusion, even in so dazzling and brilliant a book, sufficiently satisfying.

We can at least agree that Selzer is using his writing skills to understand—or approximate an understanding of—an experience that actually happened to him. Readers of Truman Capote's "nonfiction novel," *In Cold Blood*, originally accepted his masterful storytelling as a brilliant application of the novelist's techniques to the reporter's investigative skills. In the interval since that book was published, Kansans who were in the area when Capote was researching his book objected that he hadn't really interviewed key figures and hadn't done as much firsthand, on-the-spot reporting as the book would lead a reader to assume. Eventually it was revealed that one of the powerful concluding scenes in the book, where Capote visits one of the murderers in jail, never happened in real life. Capote entirely fabricated the scene. For the purposes of a novel it was an effective scene; for the purposes of nonfiction it was a deception, a distortion—the reader had been given no indication that Capote and the prisoner, real-life individuals, were at this point wholly fictionalized.

A great deal of contemporary fiction not only takes the form of first person narrative but also imitates personal memoir. This has been less problematic in the past when fiction and memoir more clearly used different strategies and distinctive voices, but the tendency of much contemporary nonfiction to use narrative techniques familiar from fiction has blurred distinctions between the genres. When reviewers claim for Mary Karr's memoir, *The Liars' Club,* that it "reads like a novel," readers may justifiably be confused about the compliment, since its technique (as well as its title) suggests it may be more imaginative than investigative.

There is some sort of sliding scale of reliability in nonfiction. If it were merely a question of the truthfulness of assertions and evidence, the reader could reasonably expect—even demand—veracity across the board, and for the most part they ought to. But there's also the issue of what the writer is capable of knowing or verifying and whether the work itself isn't better served by imagination, surmise, or fantasy.

In nonfiction the writer ought to be pursuing truth. What's the point of recording or reporting or reflecting if it doesn't get the writer closer to a better understanding of the way real events, real experiences, real lives—including the writer's—work? We have fiction to resort to if our goal is to write the world the way we want it to be or the way we would like to interpret it without seeking accurate knowledge about it (though a good many fictionists would argue the need for research, accuracy, and truthfulness in works of fiction as well). That said, we also need to acknowledge that writers, like anyone else, may have some difficulty arriving at the truth and, even supposing they do, may have difficulty representing it.

Despite everything I've said about it, there are always limitations to what we are able to learn through research. Sometimes the historical records simply aren't there—catastrophes like floods and fires and wars and spring house cleaning destroy all kinds of evidence, and, as archivists are well aware, the preservation of manuscripts—letters, diaries, journals, books—is always subject to mishandling, miscataloguing, and simple disintegration through exposure to air, light, or moisture. Existing evidence may lead us to the accurate conclusion or it may lead us to the best guess we can make—and we may not always know which we've done. This is true even in eyewitness accounts. We are all familiar with the conflicting testimony of eyewitnesses in legal cases and, though a number of forensic television shows reassure us that "the evidence never lies," experiments have demonstrated that several people witnessing the same event at the same time from the same vantage point will produce contradicting reports of what took place. The more the reports depend on interpretation, the more likely they will be skewed to match the predilections of the people making the reports. The writer who is an eyewitness to history is as subject to those vagaries of observation and interpretation as anyone else.

Phillip Lopate illustrates the difficulty of relying on memory in an essay about his childhood, which begins:

My mother was seeing another man. His name was Willy. It may have been childish confusion—I was eight years old at the time—or a trick memory plays on us, but I seem to remember the jeep he drove was also a Willys. This car has disappeared from modern life. I am unable even to picture it. But at the time it colored all my thinking about the affair. First, it was described to me as rugged, able to handle rough terrain, and so I came to picture the man himself. Second, the Willys had military associations, like my toy jeeps with green G.I. Joe soldiers jolted out of the wheel seat as the car went over the wooden runners separating one room from another.

This is the associative way memory works. It may be possible for Lopate to corroborate with family members the man's name and the man's motor vehicle and to find an old car ad in a magazine or a photograph or two that would confirm the information—in other words, he could thoroughly research the accuracy of this memory—but he is not simply reporting events in his life; instead he is re-creating them. *His* biographer, should he one day have one, may have to discover the man's actual name and appearance, the dates of Lopate's mother's involvement with him, and the identity of the motor vehicle he owned at the time, but Lopate's story, like the stories most memoirists tell, is more about the way the world seemed to him at the time. He is trying to approximate his understanding of events, because it is his understanding of events *then* that affects his interpretation *now*.

One writer who has been particularly astute at analyzing the writer's response to experience through memory is Patricia Hampl. In her essay "Memory and Imagination" she writes:

> It still comes as a shock to realize that I don't write about what I know, but in order to find out what I know. Is it possible to convey the enormous degree of blankness, confusion, hunch, and uncertainty lurking in the act of writing? When I am the reader, not the writer, I too fall into the lovely illusion that the words before me which read so inevitably, must also have been written exactly as they appear, rhythm and cadence, language and syntax, the powerful waves of sentences laying themselves on the smooth beach of the page one after another faultlessly.
>
> But here I sit before a yellow legal pad, and the long page of the preceding two paragraphs is a jumble of crossed-out lines, false starts, confused order. A mess. The mess of my mind trying to find out what it wants to say. This is a writer's frantic, grabby mind, not the poised mind of a reader waiting to be edified or entertained.

As Hampl points out, the writing of memoir is not simply the transcription of memory. It's an effort to translate memory into language and to disentangle the associations that inevitably arise from memory. The difficulty is in knowing the difference between memory and imagination, being able to determine what is invented and what is not. Perhaps the larger mistake would be to think that we *can* readily determine the difference between what we know and what we only think we know.

In a reminiscence of his stepfather, E. B. White, Roger Angell writes about the difficulties of writing about what one knows intimately. He's recalling a dinnertime with his mother and stepfather: "What were we talking about just now? We were close for almost sixty years, and you'd think that a little back-and-forth—something more than a joke or part of an anecdote—would survive, but no. What's impossible to write down, soon afterward, is a conversation that comes easily."

And even when we think we've got the facts straight, there's the writing to contend with. I don't mean merely selecting the correct words and constructing the appropriate syntax and adapting the right tone and presenting the accurate persona—the grammar and rhetoric of the thing—though that's tough enough most of the time. (Roger Angell also said that the lesson he learned from E. B. White's struggles with his prose was this: "Writing almost killed you, and the hard part was making it look easy.") No, I mean the fabrications and elisions any piece of writing demands—what to leave in, what to leave out, what to expand, what to condense, what to highlight, what to obscure. The moment a writer puts pen to paper, decisions of these kinds are being made, perhaps conscientiously, perhaps intuitively, but even the simplest set of notes, the most immediate journal entry, the most intimate letter, leaves things out, makes choices about emphasis, abstracts and rearranges and abridges experience. The writer needs to place filters on the intake and outflow of information, not only for the reader's sake but also for her own.

The acts of omission are inevitable and less problematic than the acts of commission. Thoreau kept a daily journal for the two years he was at Walden and, except for missing entries he cannibalized for the manuscript of his book, a reader could follow the day-by-day narrative of that experience through the journal. It would be a rewarding read, but it wouldn't be *Walden*. What's left out of the book from the experience at the pond is the material that isn't pertinent to the central ideas of the book. The book's cycle of seasons covers only a single year, but it isn't an effort by Thoreau to deceive the reader—he never claims it was only a year—it's merely the need to concentrate and focus the reader's attention on the insights Thoreau gained by living there. Even the plethora of books modeled on *Walden* which recount a single year in one location and follow a strictly calendrical narrative arc don't record everything that happened to the author. If it's better to leave out a character who was present at events but had no appreciable impact on them and whose presence in the text would only distract the reader, it's acceptable, maybe even necessary, to do it. Reporters quoting sources don't narrate the difficulties of getting through to the interviewee or the frustrations of dying phone batteries, background noises, mispronunciations, and malapropisms. All nonfiction writers have to decide the pertinence, the relevance, of certain facts to the stories they're trying to tell and the kind of space they have to tell it in, and they have to be selective about what they include. Something is always left out of every nonfiction, and the writer always has to make choices about what difference those acts of omission make.

Somewhat more problematic are acts of commission that involve altering facts or inventing information. These problems arise in most nonfiction. Memoir, reportage, and ethnographic research all need to disguise the identity of witnesses and participants sometimes. In writing about teaching, sometimes we want to use examples of student work, but not expose the student to whatever sanctions might arise from going public. It's not a deception to rename a student with a distinctive name, like Natalia, with a more popular and commonplace name, like Jennifer, since the anecdote may tell better with the use of a proper name but not need to identify a specific person. Either way the reader isn't supposed to be able to identify the real-life individual. In the same way, people in memoirs often change the names of people they know. One writer of a painfully honest memoir about sexual submission changed the name of the man who dominated her in order to avoid such repercussions of making his identity public as inviting a counter-memoir or a lawsuit or recriminations against him that would open old wounds; her memoir was an effort to heal herself. (And even though the memoir has been published I haven't identified her because while her example makes my case, I don't want to single her out as a sexual victim here. That's omission. Call her Jennifer. That's commission.) The recurring risk in nonfiction is exposing the private lives of individuals other than the author to unwelcome public scrutiny. In fiction you can change the names, the identifying characteristics, the locale, the period of time; you can't do that in non-fiction and have it still be nonfiction, and all of those features may be significant elements of the nonfiction story you're telling.

All of us have the inherent right to tell our own stories; the right to tell other people's stories is not inherent, but if those people are involved in our stories, we may have to go ahead. As Kim Barnes, a memoirist, has said, "If you come to the story you're writing out of a true desire to understand what you're made of and what your story is made of, if you treat your characters with a sense of complexity and compassion, disallow flat and static characters, and attempt to truly understand motivation and cause and effect, people finally will respect that. They may not be happy about it but they will respect that you have chosen to do what you've done and you've been brave about it." Kim Barnes let her family read her memoir, *In the Wilderness*, after it was finished and at the publisher's; Annie Dillard has said, in regard to her memoir, *An American Childhood*, that she let the family members who were involved review the manuscript and that she took out whatever they objected to. My inclination would be to decide, first, what had to stay for the memoir to be honest and let others see it only to check the accuracy of what I'd written or to inform them of what I had to say before other people told them what I'd written. Many factors affect how an individual writer deals with this issue.

In nonfiction the deliberate misdirection of changing names and other identifying details is less troublesome than the deliberate invention of scenes that never occurred and characters that never existed. I've already mentioned Truman Capote's use of an entirely fabricated scene in *In Cold Blood* and the creation of chapters of an entirely fictitious memoir in Julia Blackburn's *Daisy Bates in the Desert*, but these are fictions that the writer knows are fictions, even if the reader doesn't. A while ago the memoirist Vivian Gornick was the center of a controversy about the conflation of time and the use of composite characters—characters composed of two or more other characters to create a third, who never actually existed. Talking about her memoir, *Fierce Attachments*, she explained "that on a few occasions in the book I had made a composite out of the elements of two or more incidents—none of which had been fabricated—for the purpose of moving the narrative forward. (I might also have added that I played loose with time, for the very same reasons, relating incidents that were chronologically out of order, for the sake of narrative development.)" Her argument has been that these things are perfectly, even routinely acceptable in a memoir, though they would not be in history or journalism, because memoir is a form of literature. I'd add to that argument that writers often choose the memoir over the autobiography because the memoir gives them more leeway, more flexibility with form and content, than autobiography, with its emphasis on chronology and corroboration, tends to do. The memoir offers a writer a narrower scope, a more specific field of focus, which is one reason memoirs tend to be shorter and livelier than autobiographies, histories, or journalism (which of course have other virtues in their turn, including, supposedly, greater objectivity toward their subjects, more extensive research, and thorough cross-checking of factual information).

The expectation that a work of literary nonfiction should always be equivalent to a work of scientific scholarship or journalistic reporting strikes me, at least, as unrealistic, because Gornick is right to demand more freedom to shape her material in the kind of writing she's doing than those fields would allow. In fact, a good many writers who have abandoned those fields for creative nonfiction have done so to escape the sterility of their methodology, not to gain the license to make things up. As Gornick asserts, she hasn't fabricated her material, but fashioned it.

There may be fine lines of demarcation between truth and fact, or between fashion and fabrication, but they are difficult to locate absolutely. A writer who decides to collapse two or three events into one for the purpose of making clearer the overall impact of the events is different from the one who narrates events that never happened in order to convince us that he was there or that the events happened. Gornick walked often with her mother, but the events of a single walk described in the book may not have all happened on the same walk. The reader needs to reach the point where he understands what their walks together were like, and it doesn't alter the reader's perception of either character to know which walks in particular the various moments in the composite walk happened. If, in fact, Gornick and her mother never walked together, then we might ascribe dishonesty to the author; we'd be in the same position we are with Capote's book, visiting entire scenes that were in the author's imagination rather than scenes that compress multiple experiences into one experience. That seems to me to be a major difference.

<hr />

Because nonfiction is not merely "not fiction" doesn't mean we should confuse it with some sort of absolute that the fields with which it shares "not fictional" status pretend to achieve. What we need to do as readers is be wary of claims for truth, but also acknowledge what kinds of truth the various subgenres—and in particular the individual works—of nonfiction are obligated to achieve. Truth too exists in gradations and varieties, not in absolutes and clear dichotomies, and we need to comprehend that before we engage in nonfiction reading.

At the same time the nonfiction writer needs to be aware of the possibilities of arriving at some absolute truth; he or she should strive to reach the kind of truth the writing—and therefore the writer—most requires, try to avoid confusing the goals of one kind of nonfiction with those of another, and endeavor to represent the truth that he or she uncovers not only with proper righteousness but also with appropriate compassion, fairness, and aesthetic sensibility.

NOTES FOR NONFICTIONISTS: TRUTH

Because nonfiction draws on observed, perceived, or recollected experience, it centers on what happened (or is happening) and it relies, in one way or another, on research. To write accurately about a subject, the nonfictionist needs to take notes on what is observed and write up journal entries or fieldnotes about it; read widely and take notes on what is perceived, expanding on perceptions in drafts or freewrites; revisit locations, examine documents and images, and consult with others in order to write about what is recollected. This can be the daunting part of nonfiction, the part that demands, instead of simply drafting off impressions or assumptions, corroborating and expanding knowledge and basing the specifics of description and exposition and narrative on what is known for sure.

Some magazines, newspapers, and book publishers are scrupulous and thorough about calling into question all the data and all the assertions drawn from the data by the writers they intend to publish; but it's fair to say that most, whether scrupulous or not, count on the writer to get everything right. Reviewers find it hard to resist pointing out glitches and errors in a published book—a review I recently read gloated over erroneous dates for Eisenhower's presidency and misidentification of a man named Mark as a man named Howard—and failures of copyeditors and fact checkers can undermine the author's credibility with readers. Errors or glitches are perhaps inevitable—perhaps even in this book—but the writer who questions his own assumptions and fact checks the reliability of his information not only bolsters his authority with readers but, more important, forestalls fundamental problems with his manuscript.

The first rule of nonfiction is never to take information for granted. I learned this while editing an 1848 diary attributed to a woman named Lydia but eventually discovered to be by a different woman named Ruth—that discovery changed my entire understanding of the project. It convinced me that it's safer to over-research—even sometimes to the point of proving there's nothing left to discover—than to rely on the easy comfort of assumption and surmise. Those ought to be the alternative only after firm grounding in all the evidence available. In time I felt I could speak with some authority on topics that I never intended to know so much about but that anchored me solidly in context. One reference would lead to a wealth of information that kept spiraling outward and produced all sorts of serendipitous discoveries, information I had to blunder onto rather than simply look up. Had I been writing a biography on the scale of Richard Rhodes's *John James Audubon*, my knowledge would have had to have been encyclopedic; as it was, to write a memoir of biographical research I learned a great deal about genealogy, history, geography, geology, exploration, social customs, living conditions, period literature, period hobbies, financial investments, transportation and shipping, and so much more. Some of what I learned went into the text, some of it went into the notes, and much of it simply went into my head—as is often the case with nonfiction, I needed to *know* more than I needed to *say* I knew.

Much of what I've been saying may seem obvious to someone inclined toward immersion reportage or cultural scholarship, but the same principle animates the personal narratives we write. To write a family memoir, you may have to learn something about changes in your community, family values over generations, genealogy, fashion, popular culture, architecture, the fields in which your principal subjects found careers, the newsworthy events of any given day. Working on a family memoir myself, I've read high school yearbooks, city directories, old newspaper articles and obituaries, military histories, state, region, county, and city histories, regional geologies, nineteenth-century travel narratives, journals, and letters, family documents, and gravestones in cemeteries. I've also been reading a great many photographs.

Nonfiction is an ideal field for writers who like to learn things they never knew. Here are a few ways to start thinking about the need for research:

- Whatever you're working on at the moment or hope to begin writing soon, write a list of questions you or anyone else might ask about your subject—questions of fact (who, what, where, when, why, how), questions of interpretation (what alternative readings of your subject are there? how can you be certain which reading to support?), questions of supporting evidence (where could you go to get the information you need?).
- Pick one personal moment from the recent past, like coffee with a friend, and simply write it up in a detailed, descriptive way, as thoroughly as possible. Then check your details: go to the coffee shop and compare what you see with your description, ask your friend to confirm height, weight, age, clothing, subject matter. (This is a variation on an approach to the art of seeing, this time focused on researching personal experience.)

- Pick a subject you think you know and write what you know about it—a brief profile of a public figure, a description of a building, a history of a place or an organization, a story from family history. Include facts wherever possible and if you don't have the facts at hand (dates, figures, names and titles, etc.), simply leave a blank or indicate uncertainty (?; sp?; 19XX). Then research what you've written to confirm the facts you didn't have at hand or thought you were certain about.

These are simply ways of drawing your attention to the need for research, for fact checking, for assumption adjustment. In the writing you do, whatever it might be, it would be prudent to sometimes set the drafting aside and write a journal entry or a letter to yourself asking and answering why you think you're so certain about the truth of what you've written and explaining to your questioner self how to verify what you've written.

If you take nothing for granted, if you resolve to be as fair and accurate as you can and if you throw yourself in the way of the unexpected as often as possible, you'll likely come as close to "the truth" as you possibly can. Whatever your subject or subgenre, that should be one of your major goals as a nonfictionist.

12

LAST WORDS LAST

I claimed early on that I was writing a poetics of nonfiction. Now that we've reached the end of the book I need to say something more about that.

I'm well aware that my "poetics of nonfiction" hasn't produced a very definitive or prescriptive system. As an undergraduate with an English (read: literature) major and a theater minor, I studied Aristotle's *Poetics*. Over the years I heard and read arguments about whether certain plays either conformed to or violated Aristotelian strictures, particularly the concept of "the unities"—Shakespeare's practices always trumped Aristotle's theories. I also was encouraged to believe that literature was the realm of poetics and that other—by implication, lesser—discourse was the realm of rhetoric, which Aristotle, the great explainer, had covered in his *Rhetoric*. Aristotle, I have since come to realize, would have found this dualism a simplistic way of looking at the way people communicate. Given human tendencies to differentiate and compartmentalize knowledge, to compress complexity and ambiguity into certainty and conformity, and to adhere unquestioningly to prior practices, we still tend to observe those distinctions—that is, we usually ignore the rhetoric of poetry, fiction, and drama and the poetics of nonfiction. We still are inclined to dismiss an essay or memoir or work of reportage out of an adherence to rules that simply don't apply to the work being considered. Judging the success of *Hamlet* as a play on the basis of adherence to Aristotle's ideas of tragedy is pointless; judging a disjunctive essay on the basis of its adherence to arbitrary rules for a conjunctive essay is irrelevant. In either case, the literary work needs to be judged on its own terms, on the basis of what it sets out to achieve and the extent to which it achieves it.

Believing this as strongly as I do, it's impossible for me to compose a formulaic rulebook—*The Compleat Nonfictionist*. Instead, think of this more as '*notes toward* a poetics of nonfiction,' a title that hopes to imply tentativeness and imitate the modesty hinted at in titles like *Notes Toward a New Rhetoric* by Francis Christensen or *Notes Toward the Definition of Culture* by T. S. Eliot. Instead of a prescriptive manual, I can only provide a preliminary set of suggestions and reflections. All we have left to do now is to consider what those suggestions and reflections imply for readers and writers of nonfiction.

NOTES FOR NONFICTIONISTS:
LAST WORDS FOR READERS

We all select what we read on the basis of taste, interest, and circumstance. Some of our reading is required—a course assignment, a series of reports and lit reviews on new developments in our field of work, a guide for adjusting to complications (a new baby, a boss from hell) in our daily lives—but generally we choose our reading because of who we are and what we expect it to do for us: will it inform us? educate us? entertain us? amuse us? move us? reassure us? outrage us? We choose different works for bedtime reading than we do for idle time commuting or traveling; we routinely browse certain sections of bookstores, only occasionally peruse others, and never investigate some areas at all. We are always acting on personal inclination and changing occasion.

It's useful to know our preferences and predilections in reading for what they are, especially since they could erect barriers between us and what we read and limit our chances of interacting with pieces of writing on their own terms. In an age like this, where excellent but often experimental nonfiction abounds, readers sometimes need to learn how to read the writing, sometimes a challenging process. Consider the following examples.

Deborah Tall's *A Family of Strangers* is a lyric memoir, one that startles us by its tendency to use certain segment titles ("Anatomy of Memory," "Signs of the Times," "Anatomy of Secrecy") over and over, to make every "chapter" brief (most only one to three pages long), and to let discoveries of her family's past accrue incrementally rather than develop systematically. If you require a memoir to be a dense narrative, this one, which reads like a sequence of prose poems, will disappoint or frustrate you; if you accept the author's approach and let its parts accumulate, you'll be engrossed and moved and possibly astonished.

Or take Michele Morano's "In a Subjunctive Mood," from her collection of essays about living in Spain, *Grammar Lessons*. The essay plays with the instructional tone of someone attempting to teach a language student about the nature of the subjunctive mood in grammar; she even breaks the essay into nine numbered and subtitled divisions related to uses of the subjunctive. But all of her examples, her model sentences, are related to a difficult romantic relationship, and we not only learn about grammar, we also learn a great deal about the narrator and her boyfriend, as if the essay were inadvertently (rather than intentionally) confessional. It's a brilliant tour de force stylistically, but at the same time it's intimate and moving. The levels of insight and exposure Morano achieves could not be accomplished in a straight confessional memoir (nor would we be so engrossed in an actual grammar lesson).

Finally, consider the shifts a reader needs to make reading a range of books on a similar subject. For example, Michael Pollan's *The Omnivore's Dilemma: A Natural History of Four Meals* is a literary journalist's account of preparing several meals and tracking down the circumstances by which every ingredient came into each meal. It's a lively but thoroughly researched and densely informative book about the deep history of our foods and the choices we make about what to eat. In *Plenty: A Man, a Woman, and a Raucous Year of Eating Locally,* Alisa Smith and J. B. MacKinnon recount what they learned about economy and diet during a year spent eating only food grown within a hundred miles of Vancouver, British Columbia, where they live. Their book, though also informative, is more narrative, more personal, includes recipes, and is told in chapters alternately written by one author or the other. In *Animal, Vegetable, Miracle: A Year of Food Life,* Barbara Kingsolver, a novelist and essayist, tells about trying to live with her family on what they themselves raise or grow on their farm in southern Appalachia; other family members contribute environmental sidebars and family recipes throughout. Each of these books would require of a reader an adjustment toward authorial persona, voice, narrative structure, scale, and focus. Aside from the books' literary and environmental merits, which are considerable, readers would profit from reading all three books as a way of recognizing the different decisions writers make and the different destinations they choose within an ostensibly limited field. Each asks something different of the reader and, if there's anything the reader of contemporary nonfiction needs to be, it's flexible, open, exploratory.

I've referred to a great many particular works in these chapters; all can be tracked down by consulting the "Notes and References" section, which follows. I recommend these writings highly, but even if you don't read these particular works, I hope the discussions of them you've read will prompt your thoughtful reading of all kinds of nonfiction you discover on your own in literary journals, magazines, e-zines, anthologies, and books. Consider this book merely a trailhead or waystation for your wanderings through nonfiction.

NOTES FOR NONFICTIONISTS:
LAST WORDS FOR WRITERS

This may well be a golden age of nonfiction. The books, the essays, and articles in our literary journals, magazines, and Internet websites, the extension of nonfiction into film, graphic memoirs, video essays, weblogs, and online essays, the experimental and exploratory and idiosyncratic approaches—this is a very good time to be an essayist, a travel writer, a nature writer, a memoirist, an immersion journalist, an experimental critic, a writer willing to explore self and place and genre and venture into new literary territory as well as draw on traditional forms and strategies.

I think writers should explore it all in their reading, come to understand the full range of possibility in the fourth genre, and veer in the direction their writing leads them. I gave a list of recommendations at the end of the first chapter and I'd suggest rereading them now. All I have to add to those suggestions is this:

Nonfiction is a literary genre as unbounded and expansive as any other. It is capable of drawing on the narrative, lyric, dramatic, meditative, reflective, and referential modes available to the other genres. If you want to be a nonfictionist, start exploring what you want to know about yourself and about your world, then plunge into the process of discovery—find out what the writing can teach you about what you need to know, explore what the writing needs to be. The nonfictionist needs to be flexible, open, and exploratory too. Nonfiction is limited only by the imagination and insight of the writer; it can accomplish anything the writer—and the writing—needs it to do.

NOTES AND
REFERENCES

EPIGRAPH

Carson, Rachel, quoted in Paul Brooks, *The House of Life: Rachel Carson at Work*. Boston: Houghton-Mifflin, 1972: 2.

Didion, Joan. "Why I Write," *The New York Times Magazine*. 5 December 1979: 50.

PREFACE

Montaigne, Michel Eyquem. *The Complete Essays of Montaigne*. Trans. Donald Frame. Stanford: Stanford University Press, 1969.

Root, Robert L., Jr., and Michael Steinberg, eds. *The Fourth Genre: Contemporary Writers of/on Creative Nonfiction*. 4th ed. New York: Longman, 2007.

THE NATURE OF NONFICTION

Bird, Isabella L. *Isabella Lucy Bird's "A Lady's Life in the Rocky Mountains": An Annotated Text*. Ed. Ernest S. Bernard. Norman: University of Oklahoma Press, 1999.

Britton, James, et al. *The Development of Writing Abilities (11-18)*. London: Macmillan Education, 1975.

Ehrlich, Gretel. *The Solace of Open Spaces*. New York: Viking, 1985.

Elbow, Peter. *Writing Without Teachers*. New York: Oxford University Press, 1973.

Emig, Janet. *The Composing Processes of Twelfth-Graders*. Urbana, IL: NCTE, 1971.

Macrorie, Ken. *Uptaught*. New York: Hayden, 1970.

McPhee, John. *Annals of the Former World*. New York: Farrar, Straus and Giroux, 1998.

———. *Oranges*. New York: Farrar, Straus and Giroux, 1967.

———. *Rising from the Plains*. New York: Farrar, Straus and Giroux, 1986.

Moffett, James. *Teaching the Universe of Discourse*. Boston: Houghton Mifflin, 1968.

Murray, Donald M. *A Writer Teaches Writing*. Boston: Houghton Mifflin, 1968.

Solnit, Rebecca. *River of Shadows: Eadweard Muybridge and the Technological Wild West*. New York: Penguin, 2003.

Strunk, William, Jr., and E. B. White. *The Elements of Style*. New York: Macmillan, 1959: 70.

Tompkins, Jane. *West of Everything: The Inner Life of Westerns*. New York: Oxford University Press, 1992.

Williams, Terry Tempest. *Leap*. New York: Pantheon, 2000.

NOT THE DESIGN OF THE AUTHOR

Gornick, Vivian. *The Situation and the Story: The Art of Personal Narrative*. New York: Farrar, Straus and Giroux, 2001.

Holmes, Richard. *Footsteps: Adventures of a Romantic Biographer*. New York: Penguin, 1986.

Jerome, John. *The Writing Trade: A Year in the Life*. New York: Viking, 1992.

Lorch, Sue. "Confessions of a Former Sailor." In *Writers on Writing*, ed. Tom Waldrep. New York: Random House, 1985: 165–71.

Murray, Donald M. *Expecting the Unexpected: Teaching Myself—and Others— to Read and Write*. Portsmouth, NH: Boynton/Cook, 1989.

Root, Robert. *Recovering Ruth: A Biographer's Tale*. Lincoln: University of Nebraska Press, 2003.

Root, Robert L., Jr., ed. *"Time by Moments Steals Away": The 1848 Journal of Ruth Douglass*. Detroit: Wayne State University Press, 1998.

Sher, Gail. *One Continuous Mistake: Four Noble Truths for Writers.* New York: Penguin, 1999.

Winchester, Simon. *The Map That Changed the World: William Smith and the Birth of Modern Geology.* New York: Harper Perennial, 2002.

———. *The Professor and the Madman: A Tale of Murder, Insanity, and the Making of the Oxford English Dictionary.* New York: Harper Perennial, 1999.

THE EXPERIMENTAL ART

Note: The theme of Christine White's essay on synchronicity was sadly validated by life itself. After "Reflection Rag" was accepted for publication, Christine White and her husband were killed in a plane crash, as Roberto Clemente had been. As tragic as this event was, it was one about which Christine White had already said, "I believe the universe works this way." These circumstances give unsettling relevance to the themes of her essay.

Works Cited

McClanahan, Rebecca. "The Riddle Song." In *The Riddle Song and Other Essays.* Athens: University of Georgia Press, 2002: 18–55.

McPhee, John. "The Search for Marvin Gardens." In *Pieces of the Frame.* New York: Farrar, Straus and Giroux, 1975: 73–89.

Rawlings, Wendy. "Virtually Romance: A Discourse on Love in the Information Age." *Fourth Genre: Explorations in Nonfiction* 4:1 (Spring 2002): 206–26. Reprinted in *The Fourth Genre: Contemporary Writers of/on Creative Nonfiction.* 4th ed. New York: Longman, 2007: 228–37.

White, Christine. "Reflection Rag: Uncle Joe, Roberto Clemente, and I." *Fourth Genre: Explorations in Nonfiction* 4:1 (Spring 2002): 206–26. Reprinted in *The Fourth Genre: Contemporary Writers of/on Creative Nonfiction.* 4th ed. New York: Longman, 2007: 309–24.

Willard, Nancy. "The Friendship Tarot." In *Between Friends,* ed. Mickey Pearlman. Boston: Houghton Mifflin, 1994: 195–203. Reprinted in *The Fourth Genre: Contemporary Writers of/on Creative Nonfiction,* ed. Robert L. Root Jr. and Michael Steinberg. Boston: Allyn & Bacon, 1999: 237–42.

THE ART OF SEEING

Blew, Mary Clearman. *All but the Waltz: A Memoir of Five Generations in the Life of a Montana Family.* New York: Penguin, 1991.

Bradley, James, with Ron Powers. *Flags of Our Fathers.* New York: Bantam, 2000.

Capa, Robert. *Slightly Out of Focus.* New York: Modern Library, 1999.

Coles, Robert. *Doing Documentary Work.* New York: Oxford University Press, 1997.

Dyer, Geoff. "Caption." *Civilization* (October/November 1997): 100.

Lott, Bret. *Fathers, Sons, and Brothers: The Men in My Family.* New York: Harcourt, Brace, 1997.

Oates, Joyce Carol. "Caption." *Civilization* (February/March 1997): 96.

O'Donnell, Mark. "Caption." *Civilization* (June/July 1997): 96.

Poirier-Bures, Simone. *That Shining Place.* Ottawa: Oberon Press, 1995.

Prose, Francine. "Caption." *Civilization* (October/November 1998): 112.

Shields, Carol. "Caption." *Civilization* (October/November 1996): 112.

COLLAGE, MONTAGE, MOSAIC, VIGNETTE, EPISODE, SEGMENT

Best American Essays 1991. Ed. Joyce Carol Oates. Series Editor: Robert Atwan. Boston: Ticknor & Fields, 1991.

Brown, Rosellen, ed. *Ploughshares* 20:2–3 (Fall 1994).

Dillard, Annie. *For the Time Being.* New York: Knopf, 1999.

——. "Living Like Weasels." In *Teaching a Stone to Talk: Expeditions and Encounters.* New York: Harper, 1982: 29–34.

Ehrlich, Gretel. "Cold Comfort." *Harper's* 294:1762 (March 1997): 34–44.

——. "From a Sheepherder's Notebook: Three Days." In *The Solace of Open Spaces.* New York: Viking, 1985: 54–61.

Faery, Rebecca Blevins. "Text and Context: The Essay and the Politics of Disjunctive Form." In *What Do I Know? Reading, Writing, and Teaching the Essay,* ed. Janis Forman. Portsmouth, NH: Boynton/Cook, 1996: 55–68.

Gordon, Mary. "Still Life: Notes on Pierre Bonnard and My Mother's Ninetieth Birthday." *Harper's Magazine* 297:1783 (December 1998): 48–53.

Gruchow, Paul. "Eight Variations on the Idea of Failure." *American Literary Review* 5:2 (Fall 1994): 31–38. Special Issue, *Old Friends, New Neighbors: A Celebration of the American Essay,* ed. W. Scott Olsen.

Holtz, William. "Brother's Keeper: An Elegy." *American Literary Review* 5:2 (Fall 1994): 147–63. Special Issue, *Old Friends, New Neighbors: A Celebration of the American Essay,* ed. W. Scott Olsen. Reprinted in Holtz, William, *Gathering the Family.* Columbia: University of Missouri Press, 1997: 98–119.

Klaus, Carl H. "Excursions of the Mind: Toward a Poetics of Uncertainty in the Disjunctive Essay." In *What Do I Know? Reading, Writing, and Teaching the Essay,* ed. Janis Forman. Portsmouth, NH: Boynton/Cook, 1996: 39–53.

Nye, Naomi Shihab. "Three Pokes of a Thistle." In *Never in a Hurry: Essays on People and Places.* Columbia: University of South Carolina Press, 1996: 26–31.

Oliver, Mary. *A Poetry Handbook.* San Diego: Harcourt, Brace, 1994.

———. "Sister Turtle." In *Winter Hours.* Boston: Houghton Mifflin, 1999: 14–23.

Olsen, W. Scott, ed. *Old Friends, New Neighbors: A Celebration of the American Essay. American Literary Review* 5:2 (Fall 1994). Special issue.

Root, Robert L., Jr. "Knowing Where You've Been." *Ascent* 27:3 (Spring 2003): 45–55. Reprinted in *The Fourth Genre: Contemporary Writers of/on Creative Nonfiction.* 4th ed. New York: Longman, 2007: 242–48.

Rudman, Mark. "Mosaic on Walking." In *The Best American Essays 1991,* ed. Joyce Carol Oates. Boston: Ticknor & Fields, 1991: 138–53.

Saner, Reg. "The Ideal Particle and the Great Unconformity." In *The Best American Essays 1991,* ed. Joyce Carol Oates. New York: Ticknor & Fields, 1991: 154–95. Reprinted in Saner, Reg, *The Four-Cornered Falcon: Essays on the Interior West and the Natural Scene.* Baltimore: Johns Hopkins Press, 1993.

Sanford, Carol. "Always Looking." Unpublished essay.

Schwartz, Lynne Sharon. "Time Off to Translate." *American Literary Review* 5:2 (Fall 1994): 15–30. Special Issue, *Old Friends, New Neighbors: A Celebration of the American Essay,* ed. W. Scott Olsen.

Smock, Frederick. "Anonymous: A Brief Memoir." *American Literary Review* 5:2 (Fall 1994): 68–72. Special Issue, *Old Friends, New Neighbors: A Celebration of the American Essay,* ed. W. Scott Olsen.

Steinberg, Michael. "'I've Got It, No, You Take It': An Aging Ballplayer's Dilemma" and "On the Road Again: A Softball Gypsy's Last Go-Round." Unpublished essays.

Toth, Susan Allen. "Going to the Movies." In *How to Prepare for Your High-School Reunion and Other Midlife Musings.* New York: Ballantine Books, 1990: 108–112.

"Virtues & Vices." *Grand Tour* 1:4 (Fall 1996).

Willard, Nancy. "The Friendship Tarot." In *Between Friends,* ed. Mickey Pearlman. Boston: Houghton Mifflin, 1994: 195–203.

THIS IS WHAT THE SPACES SAY

Note: I make reference here to two vital works of arts, Hieronymus Bosch's "The Garden of Earthly Delights" and Jan van Eyck's "The Ghent Altarpiece," which I also referred to in an earlier chapter. Readers wishing for a fuller understanding of the references can find Bosch's painting on the final page of *Leap* by Terry Tempest Williams (New York: Pantheon, 2000). The online www.abcgallery.com has a site for Bosch's painting at www.abcgallery.com/B/bosch/bosch-2.html. Van Eyck's painting, also called "The Adoration of the Lamb," can be found at www.abcgallery.com/E/eyck/eyck8.html#6. Other sites are also available for these paintings.

Dillard, Annie. *The Writing Life.* New York: Harper & Row, 1989.

Galvin, James. *The Meadow.* New York: Henry Holt, 1992.

Hampl, Patricia. *Spillville.* Minneapolis: Milkweed, 1987.

Hongo, Garrett. *Volcano: A Memoir of Hawai'i.* New York: Knopf, 1995.

Root, Robert L., Jr. *E. B. White: The Emergence of an Essayist.* Iowa City: University of Iowa Press, 1999.

———. *Thomas Southerne.* New York: Twayne, 1981.

Sanders, Scott Russell. "The Warehouse and the Wilderness." Unpublished essay, 5.

Stegner, Wallace. *Beyond the Hundredth Meridian: John Wesley Powell and the Second Opening of the West.* Boston: Houghton Mifflin, 1954.

IMMEDIACY

Fleischman, Suzanne. *Tense and Narrativity: From Medieval Performance to Modern Fiction.* Austin: University of Texas Press, 1990.

Gilb, Dagoberto. "Northeast Direct." In *The Fourth Genre: Contemporary Writers of/on Creative Nonfiction,* ed. Robert L. Root Jr. and Michael Steinberg. 4th Ed. New York: Longman, 2006: 103–106.

Kazin, Alfred. *A Walker in the City.* New York: Harcourt, 1974.

Kenyon, Jane. *Let Evening Come.* Saint Paul: Graywolf, 1990.

Langer, Susanne K. *Feeling and Form: A Theory of Art.* New York: Scribner's, 1953.

Matthiessen, Peter. *African Silences.* New York: Random House, 1991.

———. *The Birds of Heaven: Travels with Cranes.* New York: North Point Press, 2001.

———. *End of the Earth: Voyages to Antarctica.* New York: National Geographic, 2003.

Morley, Christopher. *The Romany Stain.* Garden City, NY: Doubleday, 1926.

Murray, Donald M. *My Twice-Lived Life: A Memoir.* New York: Ballantine, 2001.

Nelson, Susan Hunt. "The Simple Present Tense of Poetry: Journeying in Place." *Xanadu* 17 (1994): 53–58.

Phelan, James. "Present Tense Narration, Mimesis, the Narrative Norm, and the Positioning of the Reader in Waiting for the Barbarians." In *Understanding Narrative,* ed. James Phelan and Peter J. Rabinowitz. Columbus: Ohio State University Press, 1994.

Terrill, Richard. "Trout Fishing: A Manifesto." *River Teeth* 5:1 (Fall 2003): 127–28.

White, E. B. *Here Is New York.* 1949; reprint. New York: The Little Bookroom, 1999.

Winchester, Simon. *The Meaning of Everything: The Story of the Oxford English Dictionary.* New York: Oxford University Press, 2003.

Wright, George T. "The Lyric Present: Simple Present Verbs in English Poems." *PMLA* 89:3 (May 1974): 563–79.

DISTANCE

Coles, Robert. *Doing Documentary Work.* New York: Oxford University Press, 1997.

Dutton, Dennis. "Language Crimes." *Wall Street Journal* (5 February 1999): W11.

Elbow, Peter. "Foreward: Personal Voice in Academic Discourse." *Pre-Text: A Journal of Rhetorical Theory* II (Spring/Summer): 7–20.

Junger, Sebastian. *The Perfect Storm: A True Story of Men Against the Sea.* New York: Norton, 1997.

King, Ross. *Brunelleschi's Dome: How a Renaissance Genius Reinvented Architecture.* New York: Walker, 2000.

Krakauer, Jon. *Into Thin Air: A Personal Account of the Mount Everest Disaster.* New York: Villard, 1997.

Larson, Erik. *Isaac's Storm: A Man, a Time, and the Deadliest Hurricane in History.* New York: Crown, 1999.

Lorch, Sue. "Confessions of a Former Sailor." In *Writers on Writing,* ed. Tom Waldrep. New York: Random House, 1985: 165–71.

Macrorie, Ken. *Uptaught.* New York: Hayden, 1970.

Ohmann, Richard. *English in America.* New York: Oxford University Press, 1976.

Orwell, George. "Politics and the English Language." In *A Collection of Essays.* New York: Harper & Row, 1953: 156–71.

Raymo, Chet. *Honey from Stone: A Naturalist's Search for God.* Minneapolis: Hungry Mind Press, 1997.

———. *The Soul of Night: An Astronomical Pilgrimage.* Minneapolis: Hungry Mind Press, 1996.

Sanders, Scott Russell. "From Anonymous, Evasive Prose to Writing with Passion." *The Chronicle of Higher Education* (October 10, 1997): B4–B5.

Schaller, George B. *Stones of Silence: Journeys in the Himalaya.* New York: Viking, 1980.

Sebald, W. G. *The Rings of Saturn.* Trans. Michael Hulse. New York: New Directions, 1998.

Sobel, Dava. *Longitude: The True Story of a Lone Genius Who Solved the Greatest Scientific Problem of His Time.* New York: Walker, 1995.

Solnit, Rebecca. *River of Shadows: Eadweard Muybridge and the Technological Wild West.* New York: Penguin, 2003.

Standiford, Les. *Last Train to Paradise: Henry Flagler and the Spectacular Rise and Fall of the Railroad That Crossed an Ocean.* New York: Crown, 2002.

Thoreau, Henry David. *Walden.* Ed. J. Lyndon Shanley. Princeton: Princeton University Press, 1973.

Tompkins, Jane. *West of Everything: The Inner Life of Westerns.* New York: Oxford University Press, 1992.

Torgovnick, Marianna de Marco. *Crossing Ocean Parkway: Readings by an Italian-American Daughter.* Chicago: University of Chicago Press, 1994.

Torgovnick, Marianna. "Experimental Critical Writing." *ADE Bulletin* 96 (Fall 1990): 8–10.

———, ed. *Eloquent Obsessions: Writing Cultural Criticism.* Durham: Duke University Press, 1994.

Winchester, Simon. *The Map That Changed the World: William Smith and the Birth of Modern Geology.* New York: Harper Perennial, 2002.

———. *The Meaning of Everything: The Story of the Oxford English Dictionary.* New York: Oxford University Press, 2003.

———. *The Professor and the Madman: A Tale of Murder, Insanity, and the Making of the Oxford English Dictionary.* New York: Harper Perennial, 1999.

WRITING BY EAR

Bauby, Jean-Dominque. *The Diving Bell and the Butterfly.* New York: Knopf, 1997.

Beard, Jo Ann. "Cousins." In *The Boys of My Youth.* Boston: Little, Brown, 1998: 16–45.

Dillard, Annie. *Holy the Firm.* New York: Harper, 1997.

——. "Living Like Weasels." In *Teaching a Stone to Talk: Expeditions and Encounters.* New York: Harper & Row, 1982: 29–34.

——. *Pilgrim at Tinker Creek.* New York: Harper, 1974.

——. *The Writing Life.* New York: Harper, 1989.

Gilb, Dagoberto. "Northeast Direct." In *The Fourth Genre: Contemporary Writers of/on Creative Nonfiction,* ed. Robert L. Root Jr. and Michael Steinberg. 4th ed. New York: Longman, 2006: 103–106.

Morano, Michele. "The Queimada." In *Grammar Lessons: Translating a Life in Spain.* Iowa City: University of Iowa Press, 2007: 18–24.

Strunk, William, Jr., and E. B. White. *The Elements of Style.* New York: Macmillan, 1959.

White, E. B. *Charlotte's Web.* New York: Harper, 1952.

——. "Morningtime and Eveningtime." In *One Man's Meat.* New York: Harper, 1944: 307–313.

——. "Songbirds." In *One Man's Meat.* New York: Harper, 1944: 282–90.

——. "Will Strunk." In *The Points of My Compass.* New York: Harper, 1962: 115–123.

PLACE

Abbey, Edward. *Desert Solitaire: A Season in the Wilderness.* New York: McGraw-Hill, 1968.

Aciman, Andre. "In Search of Proust." *The New Yorker* (December 21, 1998): 81–85.

Ackerman, Diane. "White Lanterns." In *The Moon by Whalelight and Other Adventures Among Bats, Penguins, Crocodilians, and Whales.* New York: Random House, 1991: 181–240.

Arthur, Elizabeth. *Island Sojourn: A Memoir.* Minneapolis: Graywolf Press, 1980.

Beston, Henry. *The Outermost House: A Year of Life on the Great Beach of Cape Cod.* New York: Holt, Rinehart, and Winston, 1928.

Blew, Mary Clearman. *All but the Waltz: A Memoir of Five Generations in the Life of a Montana Family.* New York: Penguin, 1991.

Calderazzo, John. *Rising Fire: Volcanoes and Our Inner Lives.* Guilford: Lyons Press, 2004.

Cofer, Judith Ortiz. *Silent Dancing: A Partial Remembrance of a Puerto Rican Childhood.* Houston: Arte Publico, 1998.

Daniel, John. *Rogue River Journal: A Winter Alone.* Washington, D.C.: Shoemaker & Hoard, 2005.

Davidson, James West, and John Rugge. *Great Heart: The History of a Labrador Adventure.* New York: Viking, 1988.

Didion, Joan. *Where I Was From.* New York: Knopf, 2003.

Dillard, Annie. *An American Childhood.* New York: Harper & Row, 1987.

———. *Pilgrim at Tinker Creek.* New York: Harper & Row, 1974.

Dodd, Elizabeth. "Cahokia." In *Prospect: Journeys and Landscapes.* Salt Lake City: University of Utah Press, 2003.

Doig, Ivan. *Winter Brothers: A Season on the Edge of America.* New York: Harcourt Brace Jovanovich, 1980.

Ehrlich, Gretel. *The Solace of Open Spaces.* New York: Viking, 1985.

———. *This Cold Heaven: Seven Seasons in Greenland.* New York: Pantheon, 2001.

Eiseley, Loren. *The Immense Journey.* New York: Random House, 1957.

Ellis, Jerry. *Walking to Canterbury: A Modern Journey through Chaucer's Medieval England.* New York: Random House, 2003.

Gorra, Michael. *The Bells in Their Silence: Travels Through Germany.* Princeton: Princeton University Press, 2004.

Hampl, Patricia. *Blue Arabesque: A Search for the Sublime.* New York: Harcourt, 2006.

———. *A Romantic Education.* Boston: Houghton Mifflin, 1981.

Holmes, Richard. *Footsteps: Adventures of a Romantic Biographer.* New York: Viking, 1985.

Hubbell, Sue. *A Country Year: Living the Questions.* New York: Random House, 1986.

Kazin, Alfred. *A Walker in the City.* New York: Harcourt, 1946.

Krakauer, Jon. *In the Wild.* New York: Random House, 1997.

———. *Into Thin Air: A Personal Account of the Mount Everest Disaster.* New York: Random House, 1997.

Larson, Erik. *Isaac's Storm: A Man, a Time, and the Deadliest Hurricane in History.* New York: Crown, 1999.

Levi, Carlo. *Christ Stopped at Eboli: The Story of a Year*. Trans. Frances Fenaye. New York: Farrar, Straus, 1947.

McPhee, John. *Coming into the Country*. New York: Farrar, Straus and Giroux, 1977.

———. "From Birnam Wood to Dunsinane." In *Pieces of the Frame*. New York: Farrar, Straus and Giroux, 1975: 127–37.

———. "The Search for Marvin Gardens." In *Pieces of the Frame*. New York: Farrar, Straus and Giroux, 1975: 75–89.

Mitchell, John Hanson. *Ceremonial Time: Fifteen Thousand Years on One Square Mile*. Boston: Houghton-Mifflin, 1984.

Morano, Michele. *Grammar Lessons: Translating a Life in Spain*. Iowa City: University of Iowa Press, 2007.

Morris, Jan. *Trieste and the Meaning of Nowhere*. New York: Simon & Schuster, 2001.

Norris, Kathleen. *Dakota: A Spiritual Geography*. Boston: Houghton Mifflin, 1992.

Nye, Naomi Shihab. *Never in a Hurry: Essays on People and Places*. Columbia: University of South Carolina Press, 1996.

O'Connell, Nicholas. "Interview with Barry Lopez." In *At the Field's End: Interviews with Twenty Pacific Northwest Writers*, ed. Nicholas O'Connell. Seattle: Madrona, 1987.

Orlean, Susan. *The Orchid Thief*. New York: Random House, 1998.

Pyle, Robert Michael. *The Thunder Tree*. Boston: Houghton Mifflin, 1993.

Raymo, Chet. "Celebrating Creation." In *The Fourth Genre: Contemporary Writers of/on Creative Nonfiction*, ed. Robert L. Root Jr. and Michael Steinberg. 4th ed. New York: Longman, 2007: 238–41.

———. *The Path: A One-Mile Walk Through the Wilderness*. New York: Walker, 2003.

Rodriguez, Richard. *Hunger of Memory: The Education of Richard Rodriguez*. Boston: David R. Godine, 1982.

Sanders, Scott Russell. "Cloud Crossing." In *The Paradise of Bombs*. Athens: University of Georgia Press, 1988: 49–57.

Scot, Barbara J. *The Stations of Still Creek*. San Francisco: Sierra Club Books, 1999.

Stevenson, Robert Louis. *Travels with a Donkey in the Cevennes*. Evanston, IL: Northwestern University Press, 1996.

Tall, Deborah. *From Where We Stand: Recovering a Sense of Place*. New York: Knopf, 1993.

——. "Whereof." In *Landscapes with Figures: The Nonfiction of Place*, ed. Robert Root. Forthcoming.

Thoreau, Henry David. *Walden*. Ed. J. Lyndon Shanley. Princeton: Princeton University Press, 1971.

Torgovnick, Marianna de Marco. *Crossing Ocean Parkway: Readings by an Italian-American Daughter*. Chicago: University of Chicago Press, 1994.

White, E. B. *Essays of E. B. White*. New York: Harper & Row, 1977.

——. *Letters of E. B. White*. Ed. Dorothy Romano Guth. New York: Harper & Row, 1976.

——. *One Man's Meat*. New York: Harper and Row, 1982.

Williams, Terry Tempest. *Leap*. New York: Pantheon, 2000.

——. *Refuge: An Unnatural History of Family and Place*. New York: Pantheon, 1991.

Zwinger, Ann, and Edwin Way Teale. *A Conscious Stillness: Two Naturalists on Thoreau's Rivers*. New York: Harper & Row, 1982.

TRUTH

Angell, Roger. "Andy." *The New Yorker* (February 14 & 21, 2005): 132, 134, 136–42, 147–48.

Blackburn, Julia. *Daisy Bates in the Desert*. New York: Random House, 1994.

Capote, Truman. *In Cold Blood*. New York: Random House, 1965.

Dillard, Annie. "Introduction." In *The Best American Essays 1988*. New York: Ticknor & Fields, 1988: xii–xxii.

——. "To Fashion a Text." In *Inventing the Truth: The Art and Craft of Memoir*, ed. William Zinsser. Boston: Houghton Mifflin, 1987: 53–76.

Gornick, Vivian. *Fierce Attachments*. New York: Farrar, Straus and Giroux, 1987.

——. "A Memoirist Defends Her Words." Salon.com, August 12, 2003.

Hampl, Patricia. "Memory and Imagination." In *I Could Tell You Stories: Sojourns in the Land of Memory*. New York: Norton, 1999.

Karr, Mary. *The Liars' Club: A Memoir*. New York: Viking, 1995.

Lopate, Phillip. "Willy." In *Getting Personal: Selected Writings*. New York: Basic Books, 2003: 7–24.

Rhodes, Richard. *John James Audubon: The Making of an American*. New York: Knopf, 2004.

Root, Robert L., Jr. "Interview with Kim Barnes." *Fourth Genre: Explorations in Nonfiction* 2:1 (Spring 2000): 170–90.

Selzer, Richard. *Raising the Dead: A Doctor's Encounter with His Own Mortality*. Knoxville: Whittle Books, 1993; New York: Viking, 1993.

Slater, Lauren. *Lying: A Metaphorical Memoir*. New York: Random House, 2000.

Williams, Terry Tempest. *Refuge: An Unnatural History of Family and Place*. New York: Pantheon, 1991.

LAST WORDS LAST

Aristotle. *The Rhetoric and The Poetics of Aristotle*. Intro. Edward P. J. Corbett. New York: Modern Library, 1984.

Christensen, Francis. *Notes Toward a New Rhetoric: Six Essays for Teachers*. New York: Harper & Row, 1967.

Eliot, T. S. *Notes Toward the Definition of Culture*. New York: Harcourt, Brace, 1949.

Kingsolver, Barbara. *Animal, Vegetable, Miracle: A Year of Food Life*. New York: HarperCollins, 2007.

Morano, Michele. *Grammar Lessons: Translating a Life in Spain*. Iowa City: University of Iowa Press, 2007.

Pollan, Michael. *The Omnivore's Dilemma: A Natural History of Four Meals*

Smith, Alisa, and J. B. MacKinnon. *Plenty: One Man, One Woman, and A Raucous Year of Eating Locally*. New York: Harmony, 2007.

Tall, Deborah. *A Family of Strangers*. Louisville: Sarabande Books, 2006.

INDEX

ABOUT THE AUTHOR

Robert Root is a writer, editor, and teacher. A professor emeritus of English at Central Michigan University, he has spoken on creative nonfiction and the teaching of writing at national and international conferences and been a guest writer in nonfiction and creative writing programs. His studies of nonfiction writers include *Working at Writing: Columnists and Critics Composing* and *E. B. White: The Emergence of an Essayist*. He edited *Landscapes with Figures: The Nonfiction of Place* and, with Michael Steinberg, *Those Who Do Can: Teachers Writing, Writers Teaching* and *The Fourth Genre: Contemporary Writers of/on Creative Nonfiction*. His own creative nonfiction includes essays published in such literary journals as *Ascent, Ecotone, Rivendell, Fourth Genre, Brevity,* and *Under the Sun*; he is also the author of *Recovering Ruth: A Biographer's Tale*. His website is www.rootwriting.com.